Praise for *The 5 Choices*

"No one understands time management and productivity better than the researchers and consultants of FranklinCovey. *The 5 Choices* provides new, exciting, and above all, practical insights that can help you cope with your overwhelming workload and realize your full potential, in and out of work."

—Dr. Heidi Grant Halvorson, Ph.D., Associate Director,
Motivation Science Center, Columbia Business School,
bestselling author of *9 Things Successful People Do Differently*

"A very timely book that fits a real need in these turbulent but opportunity-rich times."

—Steve Forbes, Chairman and Editor in Chief, Forbes Media

"As a working mom, I have a very full life at home and at work. Staying productive is an extraordinary feat. *The 5 Choices: The Path to Extraordinary Productivity* brings together some of the best principles of Dr. Stephen Covey with the best thinking of how to better use my time, my technology, and my brain in order to keep my projects, my sanity, and most importantly, my most important relationships prioritized. Extraordinary indeed!"

—Jill Clark, Global Vice President,
Talent Management, JDA—The Supply Chain Company

"*The 5 Choices* book is the answer to the overwhelming and debilitating stress levels that have become part of every day. With accessibility now twenty-four hours a day, these choices provide the methods to get the right things done, not to try to get everything done, and to feel like you made a meaningful contribution at the end of the day."

—Kevin Turner, Chief Operating Officer, Microsoft Corporation

"This incredible book contains practical solutions to modern productivity challenges that are insightful, well-researched, and yet simple enough to apply each and every day. *The 5 Choices: The Path to Extraordinary Productivity* includes the perfect blend of time management and prioritization tips, neuroscience research application, ways to address feeling overwhelmed with technology, and guidelines on how to manage our mental and physical energy. Utilizing the tools and recommendations provided will give you greater success at work and, even more importantly, greater health and balance in everyday life."

—Brandon Wade Anderson, Ph.D., Director,
Organization Development & Talent Management, Transamerica, Inc.

"*The 5 Choices* is a great summary of what we know about the brain and managing our attention. It puts a lot of complex research in an accessible, digestible, and practical set of steps that can help people be more productive everywhere."

—Dr. David Rock, Director, NeuroLeadership Institute

"I live a hectic, high-energy, and sometimes overwhelming life. As an executive for a large company, a working mom, and the wife of a NCAA Division I head coach, I constantly feel like I am swimming upstream—up early, getting kids to school, business travel, conference calls, meetings, after-school activities, and community events. While recovering from a serious horseback riding accident, I read *The 5 Choices* and have applied its timeless principles, tips, and techniques for managing my life, not just my work or time. I have had great results, which have allowed me to spend more time with family, coach my work team, and recover my health. If you live a hectic life or you want to be more fulfilled, *The 5 Choices* is a must-read."

—Tabetha Taylor, Senior Director,
Learning & Delivery, Manheim, AutoTrader

"Sometimes in life you happen upon a 'game changer'—that thing you realize can radically alter perceptions and outcomes. As I digested the principles and tools shared in *The 5 Choices: The Path to Extraordinary Productivity*, I realized I had indeed found a game changer. *The 5 Choices* gave me the insights and tools that would enable me to raise my personal bar, live in greater alignment, and increase the probability of achieving those goals that mattered most personally and professionally. The genius of this book is found in its real-time 'do-ability.' If you're wired as the type of person who wants to live an 'extraordinarily productive' life, this book is a must-read."

—Jeff Hill, Senior Vice President, Global Sales, Team BeachBody

"In *The 5 Choices,* the 'aha' for me is that busy does not mean important. So, busy is not the badge of honor, rather accomplishment of the important is. That one paradigm shift is changing my life and the lives of those around me."

—Kimo Kippen, Chief Learning Officer,
Hilton Worldwide University

"*The 5 Choices: The Path to Extraordinary Productivity* is the perfect complement to the most influential book I've read, *The 7 Habits of Highly Effective People.* It provides simple and meaningful solutions to today's paradox: it's both easier and harder to achieve extraordinary productivity in today's fast-paced, interconnected world. *The 5 Choices* can help you and your organization become extraordinary."

—Steve Randol, Vice President, Nestlé Retail Operations Center

"As a woman who is managing numerous roles, trying to meet and balance the many demands at work and at home, *The 5 Choices* provides a practical guide to cut through everyday distractions and make high-value decisions about where you spend your time, attention, and energy in order to feel accomplished at the end of each day. A game changer, professionally and personally!"

—Marty Draude, Manager,
Training & Delivery Services, Talent Development, Avnet, Inc.

"Not only will *The 5 Choices* help you personally, its practical insights will help leaders everywhere create a culture where people perform at their highest level. Read this book and get the right things done!"

—Ken Blanchard, coauthor of
The One Minute Manager® and *Leading at a Higher Level*

"The first step to developing 'brain envy' is that you've got to want to have a better brain. *The 5 Choices* will help you to 'fuel your fire and not burn out' physically and mentally. Read this book so you will be able to focus on the important things and change your life!"

—Dr. Daniel G. Amen, M.D., Amen Clinics, Inc.

"A clear, well-organized, and easy-to-use book revealing the 5 Choices that can help you take control of the chaos, make better decisions, and feel accomplished at the end of every day. It's a must-read for anyone who wants to live a more rewarding and fulfilling life."

—Dr. Edward M. Hallowell, M.D.,
coauthor of *Driven to Distraction*

"Boosting your productivity at work is within your reach no matter your industry or position. *The 5 Choices* is a fantastic, practical, real-world guide to getting your work life organized, starting from the inside out."

—Julie Morgenstern, Productivity Expert,
New York Times bestselling author of *Organizing from the Inside Out*

"Once again, FranklinCovey has created the blueprint to achieve extraordinary productivity. As a FranklinCovey training partner, it is no surprise that *The 5 Choices: The Path to Extraordinary Productivity* course is now one of AMA's top-selling training programs."

—Edward T. Reilly, President & CEO,
American Management Association

"Life is busy and getting more complex. People are working longer hours and doing their best to tend to their professional and personal commitments to achieve some version of work-life harmony. We're all looking for ways to be as efficient and productive as possible. *The 5 Choices* provides realistic and useful frameworks to help focus energy and zero in on what's most important."

—Jeff Johnson, Senior Director,
Talent Management & Development, Frito-Lay, a Division of PepsiCo.

"FranklinCovey has spent decades helping people become more effective in achieving their goals and dreams. The authors of *The 5 Choices* build upon the important work of FranklinCovey by giving the reader insightful principles and tools to stop reacting to the 'urgent' and start focusing on what is important. I recommend this book to anyone who feels that they work hard all day but spend a large portion of their time reacting to demands and not on what they would choose to do."

—Joel Peterson, Chairman, JetBlue

"What a lovely surprise to read *The 5 Choices: The Path to Extraordinary Productivity*! It is just what we need to continue to develop everyone in our organization to be extraordinarily productive. Congratulations on a practical and timely body of work that will assist managers in all industries with improving output, while maintaining high levels of engagement."

—Barbara S. Bras, Vice President, Best Western International

"This book will provide people with the tools they need to make intentional high-value decisions and maintain focused attention in the midst of distraction and change. I have used *The 5 Choices* myself and with my team in LEGO Education, and we have found it very useful in raising productivity and allowing people to take control of their own work life."

—Jacob Kragh, President, LEGO Education, Denmark

"This book is an invitation to switch off the autopilot, make deliberate choices about your attention and your time, and then do what matters most every day."

—Jeffrey Boyd, Ph.D.,
Senior Director–Organization Effectiveness,
Mohawk Industries

"Ever felt like yelling, 'Stop the world—I want to get off!'? Then this is the book for you. *The 5 Choices: The Path to Extraordinary Productivity* provides a road map for switching from a constant code-red mentality to a strategic can-do mindset. It provides the mental muscles to make high-value decisions and stay focused in the midst of a dizzying array of distractions. Don't just go along for the ride, own it!"

—Lorri Freifeld, Editor in Chief, *Training* magazine

"A timely and worthy companion to *The 7 Habits, The 5 Choices* offers practical productivity tools to help us take control of our always connected, 24/7 hyperpaced world. Taken together, these works offer us a road map to achieve better business results and live healthier and happier lives."

—John Scott Boston, Vice President, Global Talent
Management & Human Resource Operations, Kimberly-Clark

"At Halton Group, we implemented the *5 Choices* training first at our sales units, and eventually for all of our staff in thirty countries. This training and follow-up made a major difference in our corporate culture. We gained a common '5 Choices language' and utilized the *5 Choices* tools throughout the company. Now, our discussions focus more on what is important than what is urgent, at the personal as well as at the team and at the corporate level. These principles have made me personally more effective as a CEO, and I credit Halton's recent success as a company to people living the principles of the 5 Choices. I recommend these principles to any company looking to improve personal and organizational effectiveness."

—Heikki Rinne, CEO, Halton Group, Finland

THE
5
CHOICES

THE PATH
TO EXTRAORDINARY
PRODUCTIVITY

KORY KOGON, ADAM MERRILL,
LEENA RINNE

SIMON & SCHUSTER

NEW YORK   LONDON   TORONTO   SYDNEY   NEW DELHI

Simon & Schuster
1230 Avenue of the Americas
New York, NY 10020

First Simon & Schuster hardcover edition January 2015

SIMON & SCHUSTER and colophon are registered trademarks of
Simon & Schuster, Inc.

"The 5 Choices," "The Time Matrix," and the stylized Time Matrix model, among
other phrases, logos, and terms found in this publication, are considered proprietary
service marks and trademarks of Franklin Covey Co.

For information about special discounts for bulk purchases,
please contact Simon & Schuster Special Sales at 1-866-506-1949
or business@simonandschuster.com.

The Simon & Schuster Speakers Bureau can bring authors to your live event.
For more information or to book an event, contact the Simon & Schuster Speakers
Bureau at 1-866-248-3049 or visit our website at www.simonspeakers.com.

Interior design by Ruth Lee-Mui
Jacket design and art by FranklinCovey Creative Services Group

Manufactured in the United States of America

10   9   8   7   6   5   4   3

Library of Congress Cataloging-in-Publication Data is available.

ISBN 978-1-4767-1171-3
ISBN 978-1-4767-1183-6 (ebook)

Dedicated to Stephen R. Covey

CONTENTS

FEELING BURIED?

Jaivon opened his eyes with a start as the plane shuddered beneath him. He looked around and realized it was just turbulence . . . and that he had fallen asleep again.

He had been dozing on and off for the last hour, trying to stay awake so that he could continue working on his notes. "I'm not supposed to be on this plane at all," he thought angrily. "I should be at home with Kalisha!" They had gotten married just a few months ago and were in the process of moving into a new home. This trip had come up unexpectedly.

It couldn't have come at a worse time. Kali had taken some time off from her job to organize the move and he had done the same thing, but one of his company's largest accounts needed some emergency technical help, and he was the best one to provide it. "At least no one is texting me right now," he grumbled. "There's at least one advantage of flying a red-eye."

As he slid back into his crowded, stuffy middle-row seat, he thought about the past few weeks—one crisis after another. As one of the lead developers in a small but growing software firm, his schedule was hectic. He had also recently taken on more team leadership responsibilities, so now he had more people to satisfy. If it wasn't questions from the sales team, it was issues from his developers. So many decisions to make! His email, instant messenger, and text messages were filled with questions that, apparently, only he could answer. His life felt like this middle seat—crowded—and the problem was only getting worse.

He was originally excited about the company and its prospects when he took the job two years ago. Their product was a cool bit of software, and it was the kind of programming he liked to do. With Kalisha's work and his job, they had begun to look for a place where they could finally make a home and maybe start a family. "But at this rate," he thought, "we won't be together enough to raise a family at all, much less begin one!"

Kali's job was busy also. She was in retail and managed a couple of boutique clothing stores. Because they were open into the evening, she usually came home late. And even then, there was often work to do—checking on the next day's schedules when people called in sick, following up on inventory, and so forth.

As Jaivon rolled all this over in his mind, he began to feel something he hadn't felt before—despair. "Will this ever end?" he thought.

Does any of this sound familiar?

While this might not match your situation exactly, our guess is that some of it rings true.

When you picked up this book, you probably did it for one of two reasons:

1. **You are looking for some new ideas about how to be more productive.** You may actually be managing pretty well, but you want to improve. You want to manage your time better, to get more out of each day. You may want to make more of a difference, to progress in your career, to have more time for those people who are important to you, or to achieve some really important goals.

2. **You feel buried every day, and you want some serious help.** You may, however, feel more like Jaivon—struggling to stay above the growing pile of things to do and the demands and decisions coming at you all day long. You may feel out of balance and that you rarely have time for yourself. You may feel that your health and relationships are suffering and that your primary goal is just to get through the day in one piece. You know if something doesn't change soon, you just might explode.

If you relate to either of these descriptions, or are somewhere in between, you are not alone. In our experience, an increasing number of people are feeling the challenge of accomplishing what they want to in their lives. They see great possibilities, but also feel overwhelmed, rushing from one thing to another, trying to move ahead but worried that they may be falling behind. For many, it seems the more they do, the more comes their way. It's a never-ending flow of incoming tasks, appointments, obligations, and responsibilities. In some cases, all these things feel like a giant mountain of suffocating gravel pouring over them and threatening to bury them alive.

The purpose of this book is to help you get out from under that gravel, take a fresh breath, and reclaim your life. We will help you dig out by giving you the principles, processes, and tools to help you change the equation—a practical path to overcome the tyranny of the endless flow of the "incoming." These are not quick-fix magic formulas. They will require some work, but each chapter is full of simple and powerful things you can do immediately and that will have a significant impact on your life.

As you begin implementing this material, one step at a time, you will begin to change the equation. You will get unburied and move forward in more productive and fulfilling ways. You will get clear and focused on the things that matter and you will both be and feel truly accomplished at the end of every day.

THE PRODUCTIVITY PARADOX

It has never been easier in human history to accomplish great things. A big part of that is the dramatic increase in the power of technology to make us more productive.

Today's technology allows a child in Bangladesh to learn algebra from the best teachers on the planet. It allows people from around the globe to instantly see each other's faces and collaborate in real time. We can access the world's greatest libraries and publish our own thoughts to people everywhere. Modern technology has enabled people to advance medical practice, decode the human genome, overthrow governments, distribute state secrets, and expose corruption.

With advances in interconnectivity, processing power, and wearable technologies that measure everything from the temperature of our skin to the flow of our blood, the interaction between how we live and think and the technologies we use becomes more inseparable each day. And the revolution is just getting started.

Yet, paradoxically, these same technologies can make it harder than ever to accomplish the things that are important to us.

THE PRODUCTIVITY PARADOX

It is both easier and harder than ever before to achieve extraordinary productivity and feel accomplished in our lives.

The incoming flow of information enabled by today's technology fills our lives with tasks and demands for our attention which, in the end, may not matter that much. Technology allows anyone who feels like it, anywhere in the world, to drop something into our digital inboxes, requiring us to respond, even if only to say no. We become buried alive by the unstoppable flow of everything that comes our way, which robs us of the energy we could be spending on higher-value activities. In many cases, we have redefined success as simply getting things done on time (barely!) rather than doing the important things with the attention and quality that makes us feel like we are, in fact, doing extraordinary work.

The tech-enabled, hyperpaced nature of our work has impacted our lives to such a degree that people feel overwhelmed like never before. They feel buried in things to do and simultaneously drained of their capacity to do them. They feel agitated and anxious, stressed when they are working and stressed when they are not. It is a semipermanent state of worried restlessness that pervades our culture and drains us of confidence and joy. This is the widespread human cost of the productivity paradox, and it will only become more challenging for people who do not know how to tame the paradox and turn it to their advantage.

The productivity paradox revolves around three critical challenges.

CHALLENGE 1: WE ARE MAKING MORE DECISIONS THAN EVER.

In the early part of the twentieth century as the world was industrializing, huge advances in productivity came from the automation of labor. Work was broken down into small, repeatable tasks on an assembly line that anyone could do. As a result, companies and countries were able to produce goods on a much larger scale. This scaling up of production capability is what built the wealth of the twentieth century.

However, in the twenty-first century, the way value is created has shifted from the *manual labor* required to put things together to the *creative mental labor* that designs, engineers, markets, and sells today's complex processes, services, and products (like software or high-end medical devices). Today's economic value has shifted from low-decision content work to high-decision content work—from our hands to our brains.

The productivity challenge is that the velocity of incoming decisions required to do our work is almost overwhelming. And what most people do—because they are committed, hard-working people—is that they try to handle this flow in a linear way. They take decisions as they come, handling them one at a time, making them as well and fast as they can, and then moving on to the next one—like an assembly line.

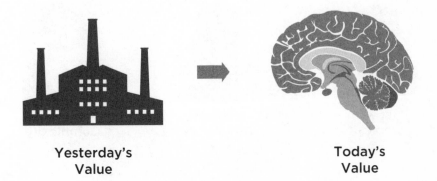

Yesterday's
Value

Today's
Value

The problem is that high-value decisions don't come in a predictable order. They are nonlinear opportunities. If we are not aware, we might miss them entirely, or only address them in a rushed, low-quality way. A linear approach in a nonlinear reality is a recipe for failure. Putting our heads down and simply doing more faster does not create extraordinary productivity in a world where value is found in stepping back, prioritizing the choices coming in, and making good decisions on the things that really impact results.

In a telling study cited in the *Harvard Business Review*, top performers in low-complexity jobs where decision making is at a minimum (like a worker in a fast-food restaurant) were found to be about three times more productive than the lowest performers. In medium-complexity jobs (like a production worker in a high-tech factory), the top performers were found to be twelve times more productive. However, in high-complexity jobs, where the right decisions make all the difference (like a software engineer or an associate in an investment banking firm), the differences between the top and the bottom performers were so profound they were unmeasurable.[1]

| Low Complexity 3X | Medium Complexity 12X | High Complexity ∞ |

Think about your own work. Doesn't it feel pretty complex? Are there some areas where the right decisions will make a huge difference in your results? Are you able to devote the time and energy to make these decisions in a quality way?

CHALLENGE 2: OUR ATTENTION IS UNDER UNPRECEDENTED ATTACK.

If the number of decisions we have to make were the only issue, we might have gotten off pretty easily. But there is a second significant challenge: While we are trying to handle all the incoming decisions, our attention is under unprecedented attack. All the beeps, buzzes, and banners that invade our mental space come at a cost to our ability to focus on the things that really matter.

Even your own personal technology can become enemy territory. If you have ever Googled something important and then, forty-five minutes of links later, found yourself watching brainless videos or reading things that had no value to you at all, you have experienced how easily your attention can be taken from you if you are not conscious about it.

The marketing world does a good job of exploiting our natural tendencies toward distraction. Think of the millions of dollars and tens of thousands of hours spent trying to get just thirty seconds of your attention during a Super Bowl or World Cup commercial. Similar effort is spent every day online as marketers' pop-up ads wiggle, dance, and make silly noises, just trying to get your attention long enough to generate interest so that they can try to sell you something. Our pervasive media ecosystem from news to advertising to the programming aired is basically a war for your most valuable mental resource—your attention. It is driven by dollars or euros or yuan, and the stakes are high. There is plenty of incentive for advertisers to do everything possible to grab your attention, even if only for a moment.

But paying attention to anything for an extended period of time is hard—for individuals and organizations. Even the language we use is insightful. When we say we are paying attention to something, we are recognizing that attention comes at a cost. It takes an investment of energy to attend to something. This is not just figurative; it is biological and neurological. Because attention requires effort, it is far easier to let your brain become distracted by less important things.

Bottom line: If we're not careful, we can go on mental autopilot, moving from one stimulating and distracting input to another, and miss the things that are uniquely meaningful—the things that can make our days, lives, and relationships extraordinary.

CHALLENGE 3: WE ARE SUFFERING
FROM A PERSONAL ENERGY CRISIS.

In the middle of all of the decisions coming at you and the attention-grabbing distractions around you, do you find yourself struggling to think clearly at work? Do you feel worn out much of the time? Do you find yourself relying on stimulants like coffee or those jolting energy drinks just to get through the day? Have you ever finished your workday or workweek and found yourself so exhausted that you slipped into a couch coma, unable to devote any energy to the other people or activities you love?

A productive life is a conscious life, and that takes mental energy. But with today's technology-enabled unstoppable flow of everything coming at us, we can often feel so worn out and tired that we face our own personal energy crisis. We can't muster the mental energy to think clearly and, in a knowledge-work world, that is a problem.

Energy management is not just about physical energy, although that is important too; it's about the raw-energy requirements of performing mental labor. Again, this is not just metaphorical; it is a biological and neurological reality. Your brain needs certain things in order to function well, like glucose and oxygen, and there are a number of factors that influence how well those are supplied to your brain. Yet, our normal work environments are extremely unfriendly to our brains. As brain researcher John Medina notes, today's cubicled, sedentary workplaces represent "an almost perfect anti-brain working environment."[2] This is true even as we increasingly find ourselves working in highly complex, mentally taxing jobs.

THE IMPACT OF THE PRODUCTIVITY PARADOX

These three roots of the productivity paradox—a streaming flow of unlimited decisions to be made, the second-by-second battle for your attention, and the draining demands on your personal energy—all have a real impact on how accomplished you feel on any day at work, at home, and in your community.

You feel it every day when you come home frazzled, uncertain if you accomplished what you needed to, worried about things you've left undone, and dreading the day ahead. You feel it when you look at your life as a whole and realize there are significant areas of your life that you have left neglected, relationships that have not been nurtured, talents that have not been developed, and interests that have not been pursued. You feel it when you think of your potential and the great goals you have, but then feel battered and bruised by all the incoming tasks and demands that seem to always keep you from focusing on those more important things.

These things don't just show up in your inner experience; they are quantifiable. What if we told you that in a world where we have more opportunity to do great things than ever before, 40 percent—almost half—of your time, attention, and energy is going to unimportant or irrelevant activities?

In a six-year FranklinCovey study, we discovered exactly that. The study was based on 351,613 respondents from Africa, Asia Pacific, Europe, Latin America, the Middle East, and North America. In this research, people indicated that about 60 percent of their time was being spent on important things and about 40 percent was being spent on things that were not important to them or to their companies.[3]

Think about that for a minute. Now, some might say, "Well, at least it's more than half!" But what if your car only worked half the time? Would you be satisfied? What about your computer or cell phone? What if only half of the lights worked in your house? Or only half of your bank account or investments were generating a return? What if only half of the players on your favorite team showed up to play for the championship game? You wouldn't accept situations like that, so why settle for less when it comes to your time?

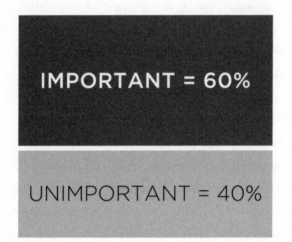

From an organizational standpoint, this implies that only about half of the money you spend on payroll is being directed toward things that matter to your organization. If you're a leader, it means that only about half of your team's energy is being spent moving forward on your most important goals.

Let's look at some numbers.

Let's assume, for a moment, that your organization is similar to the global average. Let's also assume that each person on your team works about 2,080 hours per year, which translates into 40 hours per week. When you apply the 40 percent metric to these work hours, it means 832 hours per year are wasted on unimportant activities for each individual working on your team. Let's further assume that you are a part of a 500-person organization or division and the average hourly wage across everyone in the division (senior and junior) is $50 per hour. This translates to over $20 million in waste each year.

In our experience, this is the biggest hidden cost in organizations today. It is the cost of people spending their precious time, attention, and energy on things that don't drive your most important results.

It's not just a numbers game. Think of the cost to employee engagement and commitment when they come to a job where half of their effort is not spent on important things, where they must battle with all sorts of distractions and demands that keep them from doing their finest work on things that really matter.

This is the very real impact of the productivity paradox. In a time when we are more able than ever to do extraordinary work, it seems harder than ever to get that work done. And this affects our work, our relationships, our sense of satisfaction and fulfillment, even our health.

To be clear, we're not advocating that everyone turn into a little efficiency factory, working in nonstop production mode 100 percent of the time. That is an Industrial Age, machine-based mindset that is not balanced or even possible or productive in today's world. What we are talking about is the time and energy you spend on the things that are important to you and your work—the things that will bring you a sense of satisfaction at the end of every day. What if we could increase the amount of time and energy you spend on those things by even a little bit? What if we could change the ratio to 70/30 or even 80/20? What difference would that make in your own work and life?

What if you could get rid of even a few of those annoying things that keep you from doing your best work, that keep you from paying attention to your most important relationships, that get in the way of doing the things that increase your sense of joy, satisfaction, and accomplishment each day?

If you believe, as we do, that your most valuable asset is your life and the time and energy you spend living it each day, doesn't it make sense that you should be able to spend more of it on things that really matter?

WHAT IS EXTRAORDINARY PRODUCTIVITY?

When we use the word *extraordinary,* we don't mean everyone has to broker world peace on Friday and win the Nobel Prize on Monday. What we are talking about is living and working at your best, where you bring your whole self to what you do, and tap into the talents and energies you uniquely have to offer. It means, above all, doing work that you can feel great about.

Now you might be thinking, "Sure, that *sounds* good, but I have no flexibility in my job, and I just have to get by." Think back for a moment to the fast-food worker in the study we referenced earlier in this chapter. Visualize the image of this work in your mind. It is a low-complexity position with a highly defined job description, designed to remove decisions, create focused attention, and keep the need for mental energy down to a minimum. You could argue that this is the least knowledge-work-like job on the planet. It really is, you might argue, like an old-time assembly line. And you would be right.

Yet, even in this environment, how can one person be three times more productive than another?

A friend of ours took her lunch break at a retail-chain sandwich shop. Expecting only a sandwich, what she got was an unexpected and unforgettable service experience.

When she first stepped up to order, she noticed a young worker covered in tattoos and body piercings—like many other young adults you can find in a shop like this. But when he greeted her, she instantly noticed his enthusiastic smile and the attention given to her order.

She then watched this young craftsman as he deftly assembled her sandwich with fluid movement that indicated not only a joy in the process, but a mastery of the details—like watching a skilled dancer or a performing artist. It was clear that he had thought through the process and created a sequence of events that allowed him to put forth his finest efforts.

As he finished her order and handed it to her with a sincere thank-you, she realized that she had not experienced a simple worker in an assembly-line job, but a human being making a conscious contribution—a true artisan.

What made the difference?

Even in that tightly controlled scenario, here was someone who had consciously decided what was most important among the things he could influence, focused his attention on them, and brought his finest energy to that work. Underlying that formula was an even more fundamental decision required of all extraordinary work—he had decided to bring his whole self to the job. As a result, his work was significantly more productive, more enjoyable and rewarding to him, and more impactful for those he served.

WHEN HAVE YOU BEEN EXTRAORDINARY?

Compare this to your own work, which likely has much more latitude! When was a time you felt, like this young man, that you were doing extraordinary work? where you were involved in a project or some other effort that brought out your very best? when you put your whole self into it? when you went to bed feeling accomplished at the end of every day?

When you were doing this work, what was your decision making like? What was the quality of your attention? When distractions came up, did you quickly move past them so that you could remain focused on what you were doing? How much energy and clarity of mind did you feel?

Often when we ask these questions in large groups, there is a moment in people's eyes where you can see a bit of fear: "Have I actually ever done anything like that?"

It's amazing for us to watch them work to dig up those great accomplishments. People generally are often so busy just trying to handle it all that they don't even pause to realize what accomplishment really feels like. Then, when they realize there actually were times when they were engaged in doing great work, the energy in the room goes up as they start to relive and share some of the best moments in their lives.

Imagine how it would be if you were able, at the end of every day, to look back on that day and consistently feel the same sense of accomplishment.

THE PROMISE OF THE 5 CHOICES TO EXTRAORDINARY PRODUCTIVITY

Our premise in writing this book is that everyone has the capability to do extraordinary work. Everyone has the potential to go to bed at the end of each day feeling satisfied and accomplished.

However, in order to do this, you will need to directly address the three challenges that underlie the productivity paradox. You will need to increase your capability in three areas:

- Decision management
- Attention management
- Energy management

The good news is there are 5 Choices that, when consistently made, will help you do this. These 5 Choices are anchored in the timeless principles of human productivity that we and others have taught at FranklinCovey for over thirty years. They also draw upon the latest thinking in brain science, biology, technology, and performance psychology. They have been vetted by tens of thousands of practical experiences that people have had applying them in numerous situations and organizations around the world. They are proven and they work.

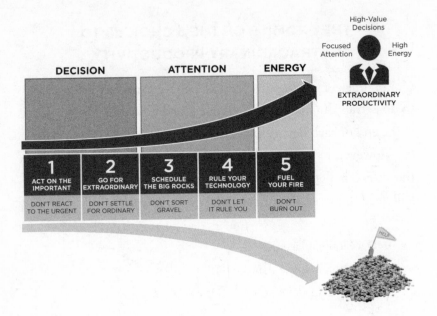

The alternative is to miss the new learning about decisions, attention, and energy and remain buried alive under the relentless flow of incoming tasks and demands—to let 40 percent of your time and energy be consumed by things that don't matter, to allow your life to be lived for you rather than taking control, to ignore the conditions that let you go to bed feeling accomplished at the end of every day.

Ultimately, what's at stake is the quality of your work and life and the satisfaction you feel in making the unique contributions that only you can offer.

TO SUM UP

- The productivity paradox is that it is both easier and harder than ever before to achieve extraordinary productivity and feel accomplished in our lives.
- The three basic challenges of the productivity paradox are: we face an overwhelming flow of decisions, our attention is under unprecedented attack, and we feel a drain on our personal mental energy.
- Everyone is capable of doing extraordinary work.
- There are 5 Choices that, when consistently made, enable us to rise above the chaos and feel accomplished at the end of every day.

DECISION MANAGEMENT

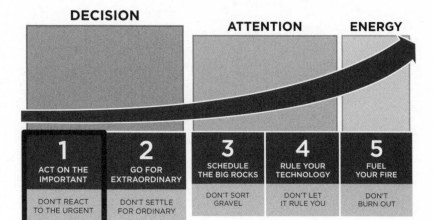

DECISION		ATTENTION		ENERGY
1 ACT ON THE IMPORTANT	**2** GO FOR EXTRAORDINARY	**3** SCHEDULE THE BIG ROCKS	**4** RULE YOUR TECHNOLOGY	**5** FUEL YOUR FIRE
DON'T REACT TO THE URGENT	DON'T SETTLE FOR ORDINARY	DON'T SORT GRAVEL	DON'T LET IT RULE YOU	DON'T BURN OUT

ACT ON THE IMPORTANT, DON'T REACT TO THE URGENT

Anything less than a conscious commitment to the important is an unconscious commitment to the unimportant.

—Dr. Stephen R. Covey

Kiva lay in bed in the morning trying to shake off the grogginess from the previous night's short rest. She'd gone to bed quite late. Her alarm pounded in her ears. She knew she should exercise. She wanted to. Before she went to bed, she even downloaded the latest power-yoga app. She smacked off the alarm.

The tasks of the upcoming day quickly flooded her mind. A large project at work had a looming deadline. And there were about a million things that needed to be done floating around in her mind. Anxious, she immediately went for her smartphone to check for emails from the project team.

"Immediate attention!" "Critical data!" "Needs your review and decision today!"

Of the thirty emails that had come in since she put her phone down the night before, many of them looked vital. Some were junk mail; she quickly deleted those. Some were unclear, so she began to scroll through them to see if any of them required her attention. Before she knew it, she'd spent forty-five minutes checking her email and hadn't even left the bed.

"Oh, well," Kiva sighed, accepting that she'd forgone her chance to try her new yoga routine. In fact, she realized, if she didn't get going, she would be late for work.

After hurriedly taking a shower, putting on some makeup, and staring at her closet to see which outfit was the least wrinkled, she dressed and headed out the door, pausing just long enough to leave a note for her housemate in the other room to take out the trash and pick up some coffee on the way home.

Ten minutes later, she stopped by a java hut in the train station to grab a bagel and a latte (better make it a double . . . or a triple?), and jumped on the train just as it was about to depart. She looked around and found a seat next to a man who looked way too relaxed for this time in the morning. She shrugged it off, reached in her satchel, and opened her tablet.

She had an important planning meeting today and needed to get some numbers together. She had hoped to do it yesterday, but there was that urgent request from Karl, who always seemed to bug her at the most problematic times! Maybe he had a crisis radar that activated every time she was under pressure. Wow! And last week he even had the gall to ask her out. What! Are you kidding? Sorry, Karl.

She scanned her numbers and realized she was missing some key input from Kellie. She quickly texted: "I need those inventory reports by 9:00. Can you get them to me?" A few seconds later, the text came back from Kellie: "I'm on it!"

"Great!" She thought, "Kellie is so responsive. I'm so glad she's on my team. I can always count on her in a pinch."

While she was shuffling through some papers, the guy sitting next to her gave her a look that was somewhere between bemused and annoyed. "Oh, well," she thought, "he probably doesn't have a real job anyway. He's probably a part-time art professor or something. Certainly not someone who has important business to get done." She buried her head deeper in her reports.

During the twenty-minute ride into town, Kiva congratulated herself for using her commute time so well. She had gotten the reports from Kellie, sent off ten more emails to members of her team so that they knew she was paying attention, and gathered the key numbers she needed for her planning meeting.

Her day went pretty much as it always did—hopping from one meeting to the next. Decisions, decisions! The project was pretty close to its original timeline and everybody seemed to be pulling their weight. There was one vendor who never got it right the first time, and always asked for more money to handle increases in scope. "We knew the Web component would be big, right?"

If only she didn't have to spend so much time dealing with corporate reports and internal politics. There were a number of projects going on, and everybody needed the same resources at the same time. She had spent ninety minutes that afternoon just trying to secure the programming resources she needed this week that had suddenly been pulled to another project. Really?

As she closed her laptop at seven that evening, she still had a few more emails to send. (Thank heaven for the train ride home!) She glanced up and plotted an exit path that would take her behind Karl's desk so that he wouldn't see her. She left the building and took a deep breath of the crisp evening air. Ahhh! If she were lucky, she could make it home in time for a take-out meal (Japanese? Italian? Korean?) and catch a couple of episodes of her favorite show online to unwind.

Let's look at Kiva's life for a moment. Is she, as she thought, productive?

Think about it for a minute.

She's working on important things—even critical things. She's using her time to get things done. She's got a number of electronic devices to help her communicate with others. She's connected. She's wired. She's moving things forward and making things happen.

So, is she productive?

The answer to that question is rooted in the principle of discernment, which is defined as the ability to judge well. This principle is at the heart of effective decision management and how we use our brains.

HOW WELL ARE YOU USING YOUR BRAIN?

In a knowledge-work world where we are paid to think, create, and innovate, a primary tool for creating value is our brain. So, before we go further, let's gain a little understanding about how our brain works.

Don't worry, we won't delve deep into advanced psychology or brain chemistry. We will simply talk about two basic parts of our brain: the Reactive Brain and the Thinking Brain.

The Reactive Brain is the lower part of your brain. It is the source of the fight-or-flight response and is also where we process our feelings and emotions. Importantly, as we will see, it is also where your brain processes pleasure and enjoyment. Most of these processes happen automatically, before we have time to think about what is going on. The Reactive Brain is also the place of acquired yet deep-seated habits. These are the patterns of thinking and behavior we've placed there so strongly that they have become unconscious and automatic—like driving to work while we are busy thinking about something else.

Scientists say that the Reactive Brain was built to ensure our survival as far back as prehistoric times. Imagine a figurative caveman walking in the forest. His survival depended on his ability to react quickly, without thinking, to an immediate threat, like a saber-tooth tiger. If he didn't move fast, he would be that tiger's lunch.

In contrast, the upper part of our brain, the Thinking Brain, is the place where we make conscious and very intentional decisions. It is often called the *executive function*, because it is where we can consciously direct and override other impulses from the Reactive Brain. It is where we *act* rather than react. It is where we choose to pay attention to something in a deliberate, thoughtful way.

Because the responses of the Reactive Brain are deeply ingrained, they take very little energy. They happen fast and, unless we consciously choose a different course of action, the Reactive Brain rules—grabbing our attention away from higher thoughts to more immediate stimuli.

Much of the advertising we see is designed to appeal to the Reactive Brain—startling motions, surprising sounds, sexual imagery, and so on. In the words of one researcher, "The implications for marketers are clear: to move people quickly and with the least amount of resistance, we need to focus much of our effort on low-road physical and emotional processing, which are the superhighways to the consumer unconscious."[1] In this view, we are simply wallets with neurons attached—the goal being to capture enough of our reactive neurons to get access to our wallets!

THINKING BRAIN
- Planning
- Attention
- Self-control
- Choices
- Follow-through

REACTIVE BRAIN
- Reflexes
- Instincts
- Emotions
- Reactions
- Impulses

The Thinking Brain, by contrast, takes more time and effort, but it is where we transcend our primitive responses, regulate our behavior, and make better choices about what to do. This is the part of the brain that explains why humans effectively left the cave and created civilization and culture. Our ability to choose a more thoughtful response to something is at the heart of what it means to be human.

The good news from neuroscience is that, with practice, we can actually *rewire* our brains to be more *thoughtful* and *discerning* about our choices. It is in those discerning choices that we determine the quality, joy, and happiness of our lives.

ON BEING INTENTIONAL

So, what does all this have to do with Kiva?

The question about her productivity rests on the deeper question about how she is using her brain. Put another way, has she been discerning amid all the pressures and demands for her time, attention, and energy to make the thoughtful, high-value choices that will allow her to feel truly accomplished at the end of the day?

The same principle applies to all of us. In order to be truly productive, we need to gain the habit of being conscious and intentional about everything we do. In today's world, we can't just go on the "I have a busy life" autopilot and expect to end up where we want to be.

To be truly productive and make those high-value decisions, it helps to have both a framework and a process. FranklinCovey's Time Matrix provides the framework, and Pause-Clarify-Decide (PCD) provides the process.

THE TIME MATRIX™

FranklinCovey's Time Matrix model is one of the most enduring frameworks for helping people manage their time and represents a whole way of thinking. It allows us to be discerning so we can make good decisions about where to spend our time, attention, and energy.

It is based on the interaction of things that are urgent and things that are important. Here's how we define those words:

- **Urgent.** Something that *feels* like it has to be done right now, whether or not it makes a difference in terms of results.
- **Important.** Something that, if not done, will have serious consequences in terms of results.

The Time Matrix model illustrates that people spend their time, attention, and energy in one of four quadrants, depending on how urgent and important their activities are.

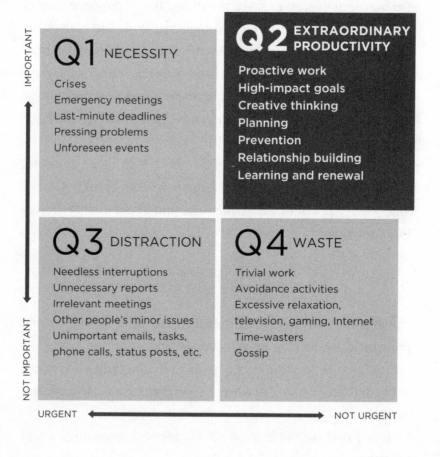

Q1 IS THE QUADRANT OF NECESSITY

Quadrant 1 (Q1) contains things that are both urgent and important. It is filled with crises (like a hospital visit), emergency meetings, last-minute deadlines, pressing problems, and unforeseen events. These are the things that need to be done now and, if not done, could have serious consequences. That's why we call it the *quadrant of necessity.* These things come at you—an angry client is on the phone, a family member has a heart attack, the server goes down, your boss needs something now, or a big opportunity comes up that needs attention immediately or it will slip away.

If you spend a lot of time in Q1, you may feel productive and energized, but if you spend too much time there, you may also burn out. Spending all your time dealing with the drama of crises and pressing problems will keep your stress levels high and drain you of your best thinking and creative energy. Although it is often necessary to be in Q1, it is rarely where we do our best, most creative, and highest-value work, even though it may feel like it at the time.

In investment terms, you usually get out what you put in. It's essentially a break-even quadrant for the attention and energy you spend there. You may even get some short-term attention for your supposed heroics but, in the overall scheme of things, it's not a solid foundation for enduring success.

Q3 IS THE QUADRANT OF DISTRACTION

Quadrant 3 (Q3) activities are urgent but not important. Because things here are urgent, they feel like they need to be done now, but really, there are no serious consequences if you don't do them. Here you find needless interruptions; unnecessary reports; irrelevant meetings; other people's minor issues; unimportant emails, tasks, phone calls, status posts, and so on.

Many people spend a lot of time in Q3 thinking they're in Q1. However, they're just reacting to everything coming their way. They are confusing motion with progress, action with accomplishment.

If we spend a lot of time here, we can be busy but ultimately unfulfilled. A full calendar and to-do list don't necessarily add up to a full life. Busyness can be validating at a surface level, but that's about as far as it goes. Q3 takes the attention and energy we could be putting toward those things that are really important and that can really make an impact every day at work and at home.

In terms of the time and energy you invest here, you get less than you put in. It's a negative return on your attention and energy.

Q4 IS THE QUADRANT OF WASTE

The things in Quadrant 4 (Q4) are neither urgent nor important. We call this the *quadrant of waste.* We really shouldn't be here at all, but we often get so burned out fighting the battles in Q1 and Q3 that we go here to escape. This is where we let our brains go completely unconscious and fill our time with excessive relaxation, television, gaming, Internet surfing, gossip, and other time-wasters.

Q4 is where we find things that are taken to extremes. Appropriate and renewing relaxation, for instance, is a very important activity and is found in Quadrant 2. (We'll talk more about this quadrant in a bit.) But when we find that we've spent ten hours on the weekend, still in pajamas with the remote in hand, watching reruns of some reality show we don't even care about, we know we've gone from productive relaxation to some murky place deep into Q4.

When we spend a lot of time in Q4, we feel lethargic and aimless. If we stay there too long, we can experience depression and even despair. We can feel guilty, knowing that our time would be better invested in more important things, but we lack the energy to go there. Although we might find momentary pleasure in some of the activities, they are really empty calories. They don't nourish our lives, our relationships, or our own sense of self-worth.

The time and energy you invest here generates zero return.

Q2 IS THE QUADRANT OF EXTRAORDINARY PRODUCTIVITY

Quadrant 2 (Q2) activities are important but not urgent. This is the *quadrant of extraordinary productivity* because here is where you take charge of your own life and do the things that will make a real difference in terms of accomplishment and results. In Q2, you will find things like proactive work, achieving high-impact goals, creative thinking, planning, prevention, relationship building, learning, and renewal. Unlike the other quadrants, where things come at you, you have to consciously choose to be in Q2. You have to use the thinking part of your brain to discern the things of highest value and then act on them.

Now, we have heard people say, "Quadrant 2 is a nice, idealistic place to be, but it's not a reality for me. I don't have time for the Quadrant 2 stuff."

Really?

The reality is that if you want to do great work and feel like you are making your greatest contribution every day, you don't have time *not* to be in Quadrant 2. This is admittedly not always easy. It takes energy and thoughtful decision making, and will likely require you to break habits and socialization that may feel counterintuitive. But the effort brings incredible returns.

Time spent in Q2 reduces the crises and problems in Q1 because you will intentionally spend time planning, preparing, and preventing. If you spend time in Q2, your relationships will be healthier because you invest in them before there is a meltdown or a critical event. You will be more confident and effective at work because you don't wait until the last minute to work on a key project. You will lower your level of stress because you'll intentionally decrease the amount of time you spend in Quadrants 1, 3, and 4. You will increase your ability to be productive over the long haul because you are taking care of your health and energy. Most important, you will know that you are making progress on the things that really contribute and add value to your work and life every day. The most thoughtful, creative, and proactive work that truly changes the game is found in Q2.

Bottom line: The time and energy you invest in Q2 generates returns that are much higher, even exponentially higher, than that which you put in. That's why it's the quadrant of extraordinary productivity.

WHAT IS YOUR RETURN ON THIS MOMENT (ROM)?

In the introduction, we mentioned a six-year global study on how people spend their time. Here's how the data show up for all four quadrants in the Time Matrix:

51.2% SPENT ON
URGENT ACTIVITIES

30.8% SPENT ON THINGS
THAT REALLY MATTER

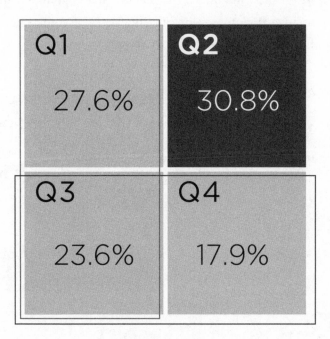

41.5% SPENT ON
UNIMPORTANT ACTIVITIES

If this were the investment portfolio for the time and energy of your life, where would you rather be investing? What if you could increase the amount of time you spent in Q2 by even a few more percentage points?

Do the hard analysis. Remembering the investment metaphor for the matrix, ask yourself, "What is my return on this moment?"

- Q1 = Break Even
- Q3 = Negative Return
- Q4 = Zero Return
- Q2 = Exponential Return

The key to extraordinary productivity is to consciously use the framework of the Time Matrix to assess what is going on in your life. It's an investment decision, an allocation of your time, attention, and energy. Where will the payoff be?

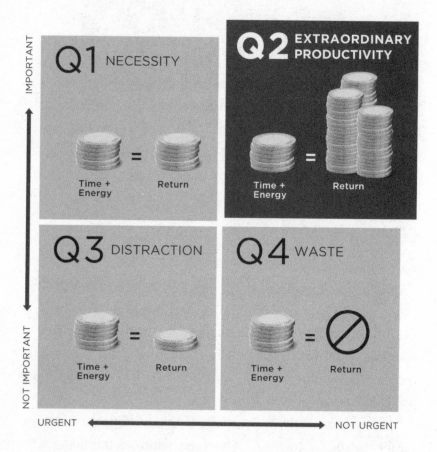

Going back to Kiva, if she is busy at work and gets a call saying that her brother has just been in a serious automobile accident and telling her to come to the hospital right away, that would be both urgent and important. It needs to be done now, and to ignore that request would likely have serious consequences. For her, this is a

Q1. She puts down what she is working on and goes to help her brother.

In contrast, if Kiva is busy at work and her computer dings because someone has emailed a funny joke, it may seem urgent (because it *feels* like it has to be responded to), but it is really unimportant (no serious consequences if she left it in her inbox for a while), so it is a Q3. Because Kiva likes jokes, if she is not careful, she might mindlessly move her attention to this email. However, if she were discerning this item through the lens of the Time Matrix, she would realize that the project she is working on is far more important, so she would remain in Q2, focused on her project.

This conscious and vigilant decision making with the Time Matrix will make a huge difference every single day, yielding a greater return on the investment of your time, attention, and energy.

LOOKING IN THE MIRROR

Right now you may be saying to yourself, "Now, this is all fine and dandy, but the person who should be reading this is my boss! If it were up to me, I'd be in Q2 all the time, but so much of my work is out of my control. If I didn't respond to my boss or others immediately, I'd get fired! Then which quadrant would I be in? My work is driven by urgency, and that's just the way it is."

Sometimes, it feels as though our work is inherently driven by urgency and that's just the way it is. Yes, we agree that your boss and work environment play a big role in how you spend your time. But if we're going to get real, let's get real. There is probably a lot you do to yourself that puts you in Q3 or Q1—or even Q4—that has nothing to do with others. Our research and experience show that even people with very tight job descriptions, even people who work in urgency-driven jobs like a hospital emergency room or a customer-service center, can take significant steps to reclaim some of their time, attention, and energy, and direct more of it to the activities in Q2.

Bottom line: You may never be able to change your boss, but you *can* change yourself. And if you get your own life in order first, you might actually be able to influence your boss. If not, you are still better off by spending more time in Q2.

Let's look at some of the self-imposed things we do to keep us from Q2. To do this, we need to go back to our brain.

THE URGENCY ADDICTION

Earlier we talked about two basic parts of your brain: the Thinking Brain and the Reactive Brain. We also said that the Reactive Brain was where we experience the feelings of fight, flight, and pleasure. It turns out that the pleasure circuitry of our brain is central to *why* we tend to seek out things that are urgent, even to the point where we can become addicted to urgency.

Most addictions work on the same basic neurotransmitter in our brain: dopamine.[2] Cocaine, for instance, works by inhibiting the uptake of dopamine in the brain so that the chemical stays there longer, producing an unnatural high that the brain itself is not naturally equipped to produce or regulate.

In a normal setting, dopamine is a great chemical, and it helps us experience the natural pleasures of life.[3] It gives us the energy to get up and get going, and it also helps us focus our attention on things that are important to us. Dopamine levels go up in our brain when we do great work, when we accomplish things that matter, when we are moving forward in our lives. However, because dopamine is involved in producing pleasure, which our brain likes, we may start pursuing activities simply because they produce dopamine, whether or not they are actually helpful or productive.[4]

We might, for example, create a false sense of urgency about a task, so we get all amped up to do it, then joyfully check it off so that we can feel a sense of accomplishment without even asking if the task needed to be done at all! Have you ever written something down that you already did just so you could check it off? (Be honest! It's that same dopamine hit you are looking for!)

The idea of urgency addiction is that we like the revved-up feeling of doing things and checking them off, so we start subconsciously looking for things to check off, even if they don't matter. We might even be uncomfortable or jittery if we are not busy checking something or doing something. We could even start to crave the constant busyness in our lives to the extent that we find it very hard to pause and think for any extended period of time.

This is a sure recipe to end up in Q3—where we spend our time getting dopamine hits while working on things that really have no value at all. In today's knowledge-work environment, where high-value decisions are the name of the game, this is not a good place to be.

Like all addictions, urgency may feel good in the moment, but when we step back and realize what we have done, we feel worse. Sometimes we avoid this realization by simply staying busy all the time. That way, we don't have to look at what we are doing to see if it really matters. It keeps us from confronting the facts about how we are spending our time, attention, and energy.

As popular author Brené Brown states, "We are a culture of people who've bought into the idea that if we stay busy enough, the truth of our lives won't catch up with us."[5] Yikes!

A CULTURE OF BUSYNESS

Even scarier, busyness has become social and psychological short-hand to communicate our worth. Go up to people at work and ask them how they are doing. More often than not they'll say something like, "I'm totally busy. How about you?" Then you'll reply with something like, "Oh, yeah, I'm completely overloaded." And then you nod your heads together in understanding, having performed the mutually affirming ritual our culture accepts as validating your worth at work and as a human being.

The implication is that if you are busy, then someone must need you for something and, therefore, you must be valuable. The busier you are, the more you must be needed. It's the existential claim of the twenty-first century: "I am stressed out, therefore I am." Someone once asked us, "If I am not busy, what am I?" An important question indeed!

When we do this to each other inside our organizations, we create a culture of busyness and urgency, rather than a culture of accomplishment and extraordinary productivity. We have been socialized into thinking that everything has to be done now, and that's just not true.

IS IT BAD TO BE BUSY?

We are not saying it's bad to be busy. Q2 can be a very busy place, because it is filled with exciting, impactful, and high-value work. Being busy doing great things is not the problem. In fact, it is one of the joys of a meaningful life. The problem is when busyness rather than accomplishment becomes the goal.

The natural function of the pleasure centers in our brain is to reward us when we do things that are helpful and productive. That's why they are there to begin with. However, they only work properly when consciously directed by the Thinking Brain. It is this Thinking Brain that helps us discern those things that actually merit our attention and energy. When we don't use our Thinking Brain to make wise choices, our Reactive Brain can quickly lead us into places that generate no value and can even damage our lives.

When we live in our Reactive Brain, we do things that take us away from the high-return productivity of Q2, and into the low-return productivity drains of Quadrants 1, 3, and 4.

WHAT DO YOU DO THAT PUTS YOU IN Q1 OR Q3?

The impact of all of this is that when we are addicted to urgency, we can easily slide into Q1 or Q3 without being aware of what we are doing to ourselves. Here's how it often shows up:

- **When we say, "I do my best work under pressure!"** What we are really saying here is that we need the adrenalizing sense of urgency to keep us focused because we can't do it on our own. Because this line of thinking leads us to be dependent on external pressure to generate what should be internal motivation, we tend to go into a false crisis mode, bringing a deadline upon us so that we are forced to get that chemical hit in our brains to get us going.

  The problem with this idea is that we rarely, in fact, do our best work under pressure. We may work hard and, ultimately, get the job done, but the kind of quality thinking that great results require is often impossible when the real deadline looms. The alternative is for us to learn how to consciously generate attention internally, naturally, when there is still ample time to do great work.

Think about it. Do you often hear yourself saying that you do your best work under pressure? Why do you say that? What are the consequences in terms of your life and the quality of your results?

- **When we procrastinate.** Procrastination is another of those common, self-imposed robbers of Q2 time. Sometimes we procrastinate because we can't muster enough internal motivation on our own, so we wait for the deadline. At other times, procrastination comes from a fear of failure or uncertainty about how to proceed. So we wait again until the bigger fear of a deadline or other significant consequence forces us to get going. Sometimes we can put important things (like health and exercise) off for years or even decades, until a real crisis forces us to rethink our approach.

If you live in the United States, when do you pay your taxes? You may have good intentions and plan on sending in your paperwork early on February 15. It is important, not urgent—a perfectly well-placed Quadrant 2 activity. But data show that nearly half of all taxpayers (41 percent) wait until the final four weeks of the tax season to file their returns, with 27 percent opting to file in the final two weeks before the deadline. Many people actually wait until the night before, standing in line at the post office at midnight, April 14!

If you choose to procrastinate, you are taking a perfectly good Q2 activity and pushing it off until it becomes a full-blown Q1 crisis. You are the one who causes Q1 to get bigger than necessary, creating unnecessary stress and sleepless nights.

Think about it. Are there important things that you

routinely put off until the last minute? Is it a conscious choice, or is it simply unconscious avoidance? What is the impact on the quality of your results? Rewiring your brain to act while items are in Q2 will allow you higher-quality results while mitigating the size and scope of some very stressful Q1s.

- **When we become accommodators.** Sometimes, in our desire to be helpful to others, we can build dependency and weakness in the relationship so that people always come to us for things they should be doing themselves, landing us squarely in Quadrant 3.

  Imagine an office setting where a new policy has been posted on a shared drive on the company's internal network. Bob needs to access the policy, but he doesn't know where to get it. He knows Steve is smart, so he goes to Steve and asks him how to get it. Steve says, "It's on the shared drive." But because it's easy to do, he also says, "Here, I'll just email it to you." Bob says, "Great!" and heads back to his office. On the way, Janet stops Bob and asks him if he knows where to get the new policy. Bob says to Janet, "Sure! It's on the shared drive, but it's a lot easier to go ask Steve. He'll just email it to you." Pretty soon, Steve has become the go-to person for getting things off the shared drive for everyone in the office.

  Now, for a while, Steve may like this. It makes him feel useful and validated (dopamine!). But, eventually, a significant amount of his time gets consumed in doing things for others that they should be doing for themselves. More important, it takes time away from what he should be doing to get results in his real job.

Now, we are not saying it's not good to be helpful or to not be a team player; but when you establish a pattern of accommodation, you breed dependence and weakness. A much better approach for Steve would be to say, "It's on the shared drive, in the folder marked 'Policies and Procedures,' " and leave it at that. If Bob had some sort of problem retrieving it, Steve could say, "Let me show you how, so that you'll be able to get it easily next time." That way, Steve is keeping the responsibility where it should be and keeping himself out of Q3.

Think about it. Are there instances in which you are accommodating others when you shouldn't be? Why are you doing it? Can you find a way to professionally and courteously help them meet their own needs? While you are helping them, what Quadrant 2 activities are starting their march toward Quadrant 1?

- **When we are afraid to say no.** Sometimes we end up in Q3 or Q1 because we have a hard time saying no to others, even when saying no is the right thing to do. It may be because we are afraid of looking weak or incapable, or from a desire to please others. It could be the fear of isolation or a desire to avoid conflict. It could simply be that we lack the mental energy to deal with the discussion that may ensue. Whatever the reason, these emotions and feelings come from the Reactive Brain.

You may know people who are so anxious to get along or avoid conflict that they will say yes to pretty much anything. This can apply to the many small distractions that fill their lives, or to large projects that never should have been undertaken. People who are too anxious to please or avoid conflict can deceive themselves into overoptimistic assessments of their ability to get things done. Ironically, this can result in even greater disappointment or conflict down the road.

Even worse, if these individuals are in management positions, they can throw their entire teams into ill-conceived Q3 projects that consume everyone's time, but generate little in terms of meaningful results.

You can make it easier to say no in a way that doesn't get you fired or on someone's hit list by having your own house in order first. Keep your calendar visible or handy so that you can consistently use it as your road map throughout the day when making decisions about where to focus your time and energy. Then, if you find that you need to say no to something, try phrases like:

"I am working on something that is really important right now, but I have time in about two hours. Are you free then or is there another time that might work?"

"You know I am always willing to help out, but tonight is date night with my spouse/significant other and it is a big commitment; let's brainstorm some other options to get this task done."

"I'm finding that I am not really needed in that meeting. Would it be okay if I dropped it from my schedule?"

"Can we clarify our email and texting? I just want to make sure what the expectations are when I receive emails or texts at night. I want to confirm that I will answer them in the morning first thing. Okay?"

"I know that I have helped on those projects before, but I may not be the best resource, and it takes me away from focusing on these other top goals. Can we discuss options to make sure my time is being used in the best possible way?"

These examples may not exactly fit your style or situation, but it will pay great dividends for you to come up with some phrases you can be comfortable with. You may even want to practice them ahead of time, so that you can feel more confident saying them. The key thing is to have the courage to politely, yet firmly, decline the unnecessary Q1s and Q3s that can suck you away from activities that will have a bigger impact on results.

But let's face it. Sometimes you need to go to Q1 or what you perceive to be a Q3 just because the boss said so. When you do this, realize that these people are not waking up every morning to come up with new ways to take you off task—they have performance pressures too. More likely, they see you as a capable and competent person whom they can trust to get something done. While this is good and affirming, as you start to speak up in a confident, professional, and respectful way, you may be able to remove or redirect some of the Q1s and Q3s that come your way. As you do this, you may even help those you work with become more conscious about what they are doing and how those things contribute (or not!) to real results. As you do this, everybody wins!

Think about it. Are you comfortable saying no when appropriate? Do you avoid conflict to the extent that you fill your work and life with Q3 activities that keep you from things that are more important?

These are some of the more common ways people move themselves into Q1 and Q3. But remember, whether it is pleasure, fear, stress, or conflict avoidance, they all have a chemical incentive in our Reactive Brain. Unless we are conscious and discerning, we will tend to move in the direction of those short-term chemical incentives and right out of the important priorities in Q2.

Q2 has chemical incentives as well; they just happen to be ones you have to choose to create for the long-term high of real accomplishment and contribution.

In our experience, Q3 is the best place to reclaim some of your precious time, attention, and energy and redirect it to Q2.

Think about it. What is one thing you could do differently, starting today, to reclaim some of that Q3 time?

WHAT ABOUT Q4?

The reasons we go to Q4 are usually the reverse side of Q1 and Q3. Sometimes we feel so beaten up from all that time in urgency land that we feel we need to crash and recover. So we go looking for some easy dopamine hits that don't require much energy but temporarily make us feel better, and we go to the wasteful or excessive activities in Q4.

Now, let's be clear. Real renewal is very important and, as we said earlier, a vital Q2 activity. And what is renewing for one person may not be for another. For example, many of the things we often consider wasteful—computer games, social media, television viewing, and so on—can all be valid renewing activities for some people, so it would be inaccurate to just lump them together and call them a waste of time.

As important as what you are doing are the reasons why you

are there and how long you've been involved in a particular activity. What starts out as Q2 renewal can quickly slide into Q4 if you are not careful.

> One woman shared how she came home extremely tired from several weeks in a row on the road. On Saturday morning, she slept in, then slogged over to the couch to watch one of her favorite TV shows. She normally finds watching one or two episodes to be an enjoyable and a renewing activity but, on this day, she realized that she was burned out, and stayed on the couch while episode after episode churned on and she neglected some important relationships at home. (The sudden recognition of her dog staring up at her with a "Why are you ignoring me?" look was the first clue.)
>
> She knew there would be consequences in her relationships that she would have to repair later on (and there definitely were). But she had let herself get to the point where, for a time, she was literally stuck in Q4. It was a painful learning experience about the Time Matrix and living with balance.

The Time Matrix becomes your personal accountability system. Only you can decide which quadrant you are in, because the labels depend solely on what is most important to you. So how do you know when you have slipped into Q4? The key is an honest and discerning internal dialogue about what you are doing. You might consider questions like:

- Is this activity really renewing? Is it adding to or draining my energy?
- Have I become unaware and stayed in this activity too long?
- Is this activity nourishing important relationships or taking away from them?

- Is my engagement in this activity excessive?
- What price am I paying in terms of more important things by spending my time here?

THE ESSENTIAL SKILL FOR GETTING INTO Q2: PAUSE-CLARIFY-DECIDE

The key to getting into Q2 is to pause your Reactive Brain long enough to clarify what is coming at you, then decide whether it is worth your time and energy. We refer to this vital process as Pause-Clarify-Decide (PCD).

Our ability to do this comes into play in the moment of choice when we consciously decide whether or not we will do something. Using PCD basically means that we take a brief instant to ask the question: *Is it important?* This simple process helps us get the return on the moment we desire.

IS IT IMPORTANT?
(PAUSE, CLARIFY, DECIDE)

Again, this is not how our brain is naturally wired to react. We know that we are wired to respond immediately to things that appeal to our Reactive Brain and get the dopamine flowing. But it is this very act of pausing before we act that makes human achievement possible. Otherwise, we would still be running around in loincloths, looking out for tigers.

But don't worry! The good news is that you already do this all the time. You do it when you get up in the morning and decide what to eat. You do it when navigating an intersection and decide which way to turn. There are thousands of decisions—many of them so well practiced that they are virtually automatic—where there is a moment of choice between doing one thing or doing something else. The skill is to take that ability you use so well in some places and apply it to other areas where, up until now, you may not have been so discerning.

With an understanding of the Time Matrix, you have a framework to help you clarify whether or not something is important. When something comes up, you can ask yourself, *Which quadrant is this in?* Then you can make a better decision about what to do with it.

If you need further help clarifying where something falls within the Time Matrix, you may want to ask additional questions of yourself or others like:

- When does this really need to be done?
- How will this impact the project we are working on?
- Is there another resource or method for getting this done?
- Where does this fit relative to the other priorities I am working on?

Asking clarifying questions engages your Thinking Brain, which improves your ability to discern.

Clearly, this PCD process will work better when others are on board with you. It would be nice if your whole organization had a Q2 culture—when people constantly used the Pause-Clarify-Decide process before accepting a responsibility, or handing one to you!

But even if your organization is not like this, you can create a Q2 culture with the people around you at work or even at home.

HOW TO CREATE YOUR OWN Q2 CULTURE

We all have a culture—up, down, or sideways—even if it's just you and your boss, or you and a co-worker.

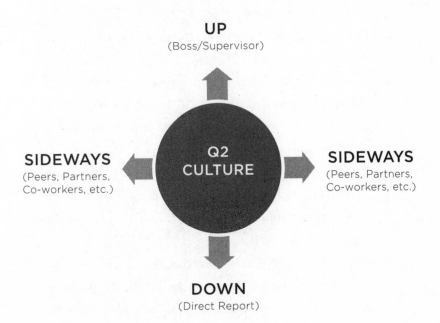

To create a Q2 culture around you, you need to create a set of relationships that have a shared framework (the Time Matrix) and a shared language (Q1, Q2, Q3, Q4, and Pause-Clarify-Decide), which allows you to challenge what you are doing and consciously focus your attention and energy on the things that will have the biggest impact.

Here's how to do it:

1. **Share the Time Matrix.** Describe your understanding of the Time Matrix with the people around you. Sit down with your boss and co-workers and sketch the Time Matrix for them. Ask which tasks, projects, or other activities belong in which quadrant. This can be a significant aha! moment as people come to realize how much time is being spent on less important activities. Also make sure to teach the Pause-Clarify-Decide process.

2. **Use the language.** As you and others refer to the Time Matrix at work, you will start hearing people use phrases like "Is this a Q1? Do I need to do it right now?" "Is this a Q3? Do we really need to do this at all?" "I think I'm in Q4. What can I do to change?" and "This is a Q2 priority. We need to spend our time on this."

    This common language helps people judge how much effort to invest in a task. When you see people emailing each other saying, "This is a genuine Q1," you'll know that the culture is starting to change.

3. **Use Pause-Clarify-Decide together.** When you are with someone and you are trying to figure out what to do, say something like, "Let's pause for a minute and clarify what

is most important, then we can decide what to focus on." When you actually say no to one thing in favor of something else, this pattern becomes more and more legitimate inside your relationships and immediate work culture.

When working with others, you will have to find ways of asking these questions that feel natural to you; this may take some practice, but it is well worth the effort.

IF YOU ARE THE BOSS

If you are the leader of a team, you have an obligation to help people focus on what is most important. That is your job. The good news is that you also have a disproportionate impact on your team's culture. For instance, if you were to take some time in a team meeting and teach the Time Matrix along with the Pause-Clarify-Decide process, and give some sample clarifying questions that would be relevant to your team, you will have set a powerful foundation to move your team into Q2.

If you follow through and allow people to challenge and reorganize what they are currently doing, your Q2 culture will become real. If you do not allow people to change their focus, it will be a cause for disillusionment and dismay. Even worse, if you go around pitching Q1 and Q3 bombs at everybody, don't be surprised when they roll their eyes (literally or figuratively) when you ask them to focus on your goals.

Part of being a leader is to recognize your own responsibility for your team culture. If you are serious about getting into Q2, here are some questions you might ask yourself:

1. Are my team's goals and priorities clear to everyone?

2. What am I doing (lack of planning, preparation, etc.) that puts people in crisis mode? (Q1)

3. Am I asking people to do things others should be doing? (Q3)

4. Are there reports, processes, or systems that are outdated and no longer necessary but are taking up people's time? (Q4)

5. Do I create a safe environment where people can challenge and change what we are doing in order to better achieve our goals?

6. Do I encourage people on my team to pause and clarify the value and impact of a new project or assignment before diving in to get it done?

IF YOU ARE NOT THE BOSS

If you are not the leader of your team, don't worry. You can create a Q2 culture among the people you work with, even with your boss, as the following story illustrates.

Laura had one of those difficult bosses. He kept lobbing stuff at her until, finally, it became too much. She realized that something would have to change, or she would have to leave, explode, or both! So she sat down with her boss and asked for his help in determining the priority of all the things he had assigned her. She suggested they use the Time Matrix as a way to categorize the things she was working on.

As they went through her assignments, the boss put everything in Q1, meaning that everything was important and everything had to be done now!

But the boss was no fool. When he saw the list, he began to

realize that Laura wouldn't be able to effectively work on every task he had given her. So, together, they decided which quadrants the tasks should be assigned to, focusing on Q2.

They used clarifying questions like "When does this really need to be done?" "What's the potential impact of this activity on our financial performance?" and "What if we didn't do this until next month?" They were then able to create a plan that worked better for both Laura and her boss.

It didn't stop there. Laura's boss began to use the language with her and others on her team. In just a few short months, they had a framework—the Time Matrix—and a common language that helped them make better choices.

Laura took this approach with a couple of her own peers as well, with similar results.

While your own efforts to establish a Q2 culture may progress differently, our experience is that people will readily accept the framework and language when they see how it will benefit them.

Spending some time to establish the mindset of importance in your immediate work relationships can have a tremendous impact on your own ability to control where you spend your time and energy.

RETURNING TO KIVA—IS SHE PRODUCTIVE?

We started this chapter with a look at Kiva's day, then posed the question, "Is she productive?"

Even though we've only covered Choice 1, we are in a good position to analyze a few of the activities during her day and determine whether they were in Q2. Let's also see where some Q2 thinking might help her change the game.

- **The Morning Email.** Instead of getting up and exercising as she had planned, Kiva rolled over and grabbed her smartphone, dealt with emails from the night before, checked a few off to get some dopamine flowing, and then, forty-five minutes later, started her day in a rush. This activity seems more like Q3.

- **Wrinkled Clothes.** This may be a small item and, in the final analysis, may not be that important to the quality of her day (unless she had a big client meeting), but how many of us have had this unnecessary stress in the morning? Clothes that had been cleaned and pressed ahead of time would have put her into Q2; instead, she's in Q1, trying to find out how to minimize a fashion error.

- **The Rushed Breakfast.** While a coffee and a bagel pass as breakfast for many of us, there are better ways to manage our sources of physical and mental energy throughout the day. This is important, because this energy fuels our ability to do everything else. Taking good care of yourself is definitely a Q2 activity.

- **The Numbers for the Meeting.** While Kiva intended to have the numbers ready the day before, an urgent request from Karl derailed her. Because we don't know if that request was important or merely urgent, we don't know if Kiva could have postponed or even declined to work on it. The skills from this chapter could have helped Kiva act on the important instead of react to the urgent.

  Regardless, she was not able to prepare adequately and created a Q1 need for information that she had to pass off to Kellie. Lucky that Kellie was there for her this time.

- **The So-Called Part-Time Art Professor.** Was he truly a nonentity compared to Kiva's über-busy life? Or was he just organized enough that he had the freedom to choose a relaxed commute to work in the morning? If so, he's in Q2 and Kiva looks more like she's in Q1.

- **The On-Time Project.** At a high level, this looks like it's progressing in Q2. The project is on time and people seem to be delivering what needs to be done. Not knowing any more details, we'll assume the best.

- **The Troublesome Vendor.** There are, of course, occasions when vendors are just incompetent. However, what is it about this relationship that, if addressed in a Q2 way, might be improved? Could it be that Kiva's team never really scoped out the Web component ahead of time so that the vendor could prepare a reliable bid? Could there be some pattern of communication that would make the development flow more smoothly? Is Kiva's team simply reacting to other stakeholders and saying yes to every idea, regardless of its impact on the original scope and timeline?

  Scheduling time to plan, prepare, communicate, and strengthen an important vendor relationship makes it possible to accomplish the kinds of activities that are smack-dab in the middle of Q2. And taking time to do these things early could prevent a potentially devastating Q1 crisis in the future that could threaten Kiva's project.

- **Corporate Reports, Internal Politics, and Limited Resources.** This kind of stuff is part of every organization. People need data, and there are always different people with different needs and agendas. The degree to which getting the data interferes with the important work that needs to be done (instead of supporting it) is an indicator of where the culture is on the Time Matrix. If it dominates a lot of people's time and keeps them from doing important work, then the culture is probably more in Q3 than Q2.

Q2 cultures allow for open dialogue about whether or not reports are even necessary. They also provide a way to talk about competing-resource needs. In terms of the programming resources, Kiva might have had a conversation that started something like this: "My need is important and urgent. Can I keep these resources scheduled for this week if I guarantee you will have them next week?"

- **Headed for Home.** When Kiva exits the office, what she does on the way home, what she eats, and what she does when she gets there are really her personal choices. Her activities could be in Quadrants 1, 2, 3, or 4. The key question would be this: If Kiva were to step back and look at the quality of her evening, would she say it contributed to her highest goals and priorities for herself? Was she feeling satisfied and fulfilled in the areas of her life outside of work? If so, then she's in Q2. If not, she may want to rethink how these areas of her life are playing out.

To experience better results, Kiva doesn't need to be perfect or reach some unattainable level of productivity. She just needs to change her thinking, then modify one or two things at a time. If she uses the framework of the Time Matrix and the Pause-Clarify-Decide process to be more discerning, before she knows it, she will have moved much more of her time into Q2.

SIMPLE WAYS TO GET STARTED

You can begin applying the principles and practices of Choice 1: Act on the Important, Don't React to the Urgent by taking any of the following simple actions. Pick the ones that work best for you.

- Make a copy of the Time Matrix and stick it on your desk or wall as a reminder to focus on Q2.
- Make a 3″ × 5″ card with seven boxes labeled with the days of the week. Commit to consciously using the Pause-Clarify-Decide process at least once each day. When you do, put a check mark or even a gold-star sticker (more dopamine!) in that day's box. When you complete the card, buy yourself a treat and celebrate your success.
- Make a list of clarifying questions you would feel comfortable asking yourself or others and practice them in a mirror.
- Post this question on a sticky note on your computer screen: "What is your return on this moment?"
- Take a couple of minutes in the morning and identify the one or two things that are your most important Q2 activities for that day. Write them on a piece of paper and slip it into your pocket. At the end of the day, look at them and see if you got them done. If not, ask yourself why.
- Identify a self-imposed Q3 distraction and make a strategy to deal with it.

TO SUM UP

- There are two basic parts of our brain: the Thinking Brain and the Reactive Brain.
- The results we achieve in our lives are impacted by our discernment.
- With practice, we can rewire our brain to become more discerning and less reactive.
- Becoming more discerning requires both a framework (FranklinCovey's Time Matrix) and a process (Pause-Clarify-Decide, or PCD).
- To be truly productive, we should minimize the time we spend in Q1 and Q3, eliminate entirely the time we spend in Q4, and maximize the time we invest in Q2.
- Remove any self-imposed activities in Quadrants 1, 3, and 4, reclaiming that time to invest in Q2.
- We can create a Q2 culture by speaking the language of importance and improve our ability to focus on Q2 together.

DECISION MANAGEMENT

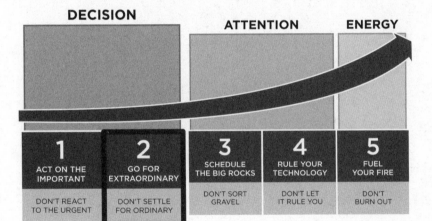

DECISION

ATTENTION

ENERGY

1	2	3	4	5
ACT ON THE IMPORTANT	GO FOR EXTRAORDINARY	SCHEDULE THE BIG ROCKS	RULE YOUR TECHNOLOGY	FUEL YOUR FIRE
DON'T REACT TO THE URGENT	DON'T SETTLE FOR ORDINARY	DON'T SORT GRAVEL	DON'T LET IT RULE YOU	DON'T BURN OUT

GO FOR EXTRAORDINARY, DON'T SETTLE FOR ORDINARY

Every life has the potential to be lived deeply.

—William Powers

Javion sighed as he got into the cab. He could finally relax a bit, now that the meeting was over and he was on his way home. "The meeting went well enough," he thought to himself. "After all, I know the system better than anybody." But he was always a little frustrated at the time it took to help people understand things that should be pretty obvious. "If only we had the time to document this stuff and spend some more time on the user interface, we could remove many of these issues," he thought.

As he mulled this over, his frustration only increased. He could see so many ways to improve the software to make it easier for customers, but with the pace of development and the need to close sales, they were spending all their time as a development team just keeping up with major requests. It felt like his role was becoming one of fixer and damage control. There seemed to be no time left for the kind of quality finessing that this kind of development would entail and which he knew he was capable of. "We're settling for good, when we could be doing something great. Eventually, our customers will catch on and we'll be forced to deal with it."

He grabbed his phone to text Kalisha that he was on his way home. She had a late night scheduled for inventory, and he hoped she would be done by the time he arrived. "Glad your meeting went well," she texted. "Inventory is a mess. I may have to stay late tomorrow night too. :-(." Javion slumped in his seat. Tomorrow they were planning on going out to have a nice dinner, but that hope had just vaporized.

When were they going to find the time to do the things that made their marriage great? At this rate, I might as well be a bachelor! "We used to do all kinds of fun things together. What happened?" he wondered. "I've got to get a better handle on this!"

To get our lives into Q2, we need to know what is ultimately important to us. We need some criteria to guide our decisions about where we spend our time, attention, and energy. That's what Choice 2 is all about. It's about clarifying the criteria for the decisions we make every day. It's about what lies in Q2 for the most important aspects of our lives as a whole—our work, key relationships, money, family, friends, even our hobbies and interests—and how to make them extraordinary.

According to brain expert Dr. Daniel Amen, "To harness your brain's power, it needs direction and vision. It needs a blueprint."[1]

WHY GO FOR EXTRAORDINARY?

People often say to us: "I don't want to be extraordinary; I just want to be able to live a normal, peaceful life!"

With all the challenges of life and all we have on our plates, it's a legitimate question to ask why we should set the standard at extraordinary.

Let's recall what we mean by *extraordinary*. It's about going to bed at the end of each day feeling satisfied and accomplished. It's about accomplishing those things that add the most value to your work and your life.

When we use the word *extraordinary,* we do *not* mean:

- An unattainable, perfectionist standard that you feel guilt-tripped into trying to achieve.
- Someone else's definition of what your days and life should be.
- Accommodating everyone else's every whim instead of what matters to you.
- That you need to stand out in comparison to, or in competition with, others.

We are simply talking about the things that you deeply feel will create the most value in your life right now.

Why, then, do we use the word *extraordinary*? This implies something beyond the ordinary, doesn't it?

Yes. It does.

In our experience, many people do not take the time to clarify what is most important to them and, as the Time Matrix data show, they do not end up spending their time on those things. Instead of making conscious decisions based on the clarity of what is important, they are hijacked by what is urgent.

As a result, they do not have a solid sense of satisfaction at the end of each day. Instead, they feel a sense of unease and incompleteness about their lives and what they are doing. They are left wondering how they could be so busy and still feel like they did not get anything done. As discussed in Choice 1, they often try to drown out those feelings by increasing the busyness of their lives.

Helping you define this richness, and consistently and consciously achieve it, is what this book is about. And at the heart of it is the work we will do in Choice 2.

WHAT ARE THE MOST IMPORTANT ROLES IN YOUR LIFE TODAY?

Roles are where life happens. It's where we build relationships, where all the activities that make us human go on.

Roles are so fundamental to human identity that when we ask people to tell us about themselves, they always answer in terms of roles: "I am an engineer." "I am Jane's spouse." "I'm a triathlete." "I am a friend." Even when people give a list of personality traits, such as "I am shy," or "I am a fun-loving person," those traits are always acted out in the context of roles.

The trick is to keep them all in balance. The way each of your roles plays out in your life affects all your other roles. If you are having a difficult time at work, for example, it can affect your mood and behavior at home. Conversely, when something is going wrong in your personal life, it makes it harder to succeed at work or in other roles.

Our brains naturally organize information in categories like roles, so organizing your life in terms of roles makes a lot of sense.

How many roles do you have in your life right now? Ten? Fifteen? Are you a manager? A co-worker? A project leader? A parent? A daughter? A son? A sibling? A neighbor? A volunteer? An activist? An architect? An artist? An athlete? A naturalist? A coach? A partner? A friend? What about your role to take care of yourself? What are the different roles and relationships you have? Can you really be extraordinary in all those roles?

One of the most effective Q2 things you can do is to narrow your focus. Take the time to identify the few most important roles in your life *today,* evaluate how you think you are doing in each of them, then define what success looks like in each role. This will give your brain the targets it needs to greatly enhance the decisions you make every day.

IDENTIFYING YOUR ROLES

Here's how Kiva might begin to identify her most important current roles:

- Project Manager
- Friend
- Housemate
- Photographer
- Daughter

Jaivon might pick these as his most important current roles:

- Husband
- Software Developer
- Team Leader
- Neighbor

For another example, a woman named Sherry might define hers this way:

- Mother to Three Children
- Spouse to Jim
- Personal Health
- Department Manager

These three people may have many other roles in their lives, and they are not tossing them away—they are just putting them on the sidelines. They have asked themselves what are the few most important roles they need to concentrate on right now to make the highest contribution.

The next thing they did was put their roles into a *Life Wheel.* This is a visualization of our roles being interconnected as parts of a whole person.

Here's how these wheels look for each of these individuals:

KIVA

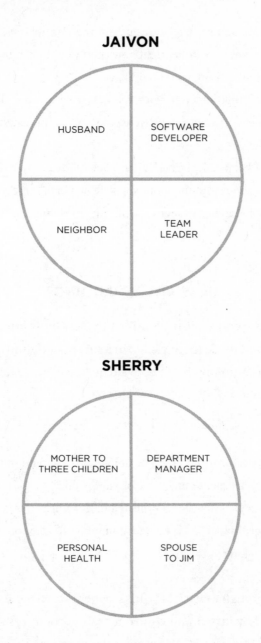

When you've successfully identified your most important Q2 Roles, they will:

- Represent your key relationships and responsibilities.
- Be relevant to your life right now (not sometime in the future, or roles you think you should have).
- Be meaningful to you. Your roles are where you will express your deepest values, highest aspirations, and greatest contributions.
- Give a balanced perspective to your life (e.g., they shouldn't just be about work or about your life outside of work).
- Be limited to five to seven maximum.

HOW ARE YOU DOING?

After you have consciously identified the few most important roles in your life and made them visible in a Life Wheel, the next big step is to use your Thinking Brain to evaluate how you are doing in each of these roles today.

Are you:

- **Underperforming?** "I'm not doing what I should in this role and haven't spent much time or energy on it."
- **Ordinary?** "I do what is expected in this role."
- **Extraordinary?** "I am excited about the valuable contribution I am making in this role."

This is a tough one, right? This is where you need to put a mirror in front of yourself and confront reality. You can see here how our three examples might complete the exercise. They would put dots on the continuum showing where they feel they are, and then connect the dots.

SHERRY

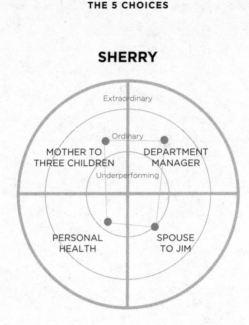

This spidergram exercise is visceral. It visually and concretely tells you what you intuitively sort of know in the back of your mind. It makes it real for you. What are you thinking as you look at this map of your current life's performance? What are your head and heart telling you as you ponder what you see?

Here are some helpful tips:

- **Celebrate.** Make sure you celebrate those roles where you think you are doing well. You should be proud.
- **Assess.** Take a courageous look at the roles where you admit to yourself that you are lacking. View things holistically. How do you see the interaction between your work and your personal life? Are they in balance, or are they out of whack? Is your greatness in one role too great because it is taking time, attention, and energy away from another really important role?

- **Validate.** Are you sure about the rating you gave yourself? Should you ask someone? We have seen people rate themselves as extraordinary husbands, wives, or significant others, only to have their bubble burst when they asked their partner what he or she thought—a healthy dose of reality, right? You might also find that others think you are doing a lot better than you think you are. That's good to know too. Go as far as you want with this. Checking in with others at work or at home can be helpful to understand your impact and how you may need or want to improve.

This exercise of labeling and reappraising is a key brain exercise that will bring you results. This may be a hard exercise to do, but with the busyness of the day, this most important work often gets neglected. Because most of us think we have some idea of how we are doing in these roles, it is often easier to go on autopilot and ignore the need to take an honest look. Leveraging the brain science behind this labeling and reappraisal work in Choice 2 will help create the clear targets the brain desperately craves in order to help you achieve better results.

IF YOU SUDDENLY FIND YOURSELF DEPRESSED ABOUT THIS EXERCISE

Sometimes an honest self-appraisal may leave some people feeling depressed about their lives. If this sounds like you, here are some thoughts:

- **Don't be too hard on yourself.** Our brains tend to quickly focus on the "not good" in our lives. Even in the midst of many good things, sometimes we focus on the one bad thing and see total failure. If you find yourself feeling this way, take a deep breath and step back for a more balanced perspective.

- **Don't ignore these feelings either.** If you really are underperforming in a role you care about, this exercise can provide the needed catalyst for change. Look at it this way: Now that you have courageously admitted it, you can act; before, you were just brushing those feelings aside.
- **Have some hope.** The rest of the material in the book is designed to help you feel much better about how you are doing in these roles. Keep moving forward, and the next time you do this exercise, your experience will be much more positive.

Regularly assessing our roles can give us the needed insight to change them when necessary.

A woman came up during a break in one of our Work Sessions. She'd had a profound experience and wanted to share. She said, "Until a few weeks ago, I had a role as a caregiver to my aging mother. But now, she has passed away." She paused for a moment, then continued, "Since my mom died, I have been feeling a void. She needed so much from me that I neglected some other important roles in my life. Now I know what to do to refill them. I also realize that I have a couple of roles that I have been keeping on the sidelines, and that I can bring these roles in and really complete my Life Wheel."

This exercise can also strengthen our resolve to keep things in the right balance.

Rita, one of our associates, has been a great example of how to balance excellent professional work with her role as a mother. She is a project manager in one of our client-facing groups and has set up an arrangement where she works part-time. Because she is so good at what she does, she has made this work for the company. She only takes on one or two client projects at a time and has built a skillset that enables her to clearly communicate time expectations so that she can work while the kids are at school. When her kids come home in the afternoon, she virtually goes dark and is unreachable for several hours. Then, when the kids go to bed, she comes back on and works in the evenings. Because she has a clear definition of what she wants to achieve in each role, and has built up some skills and systems around them, she has been able to create a balance that leaves her feeling effective and fulfilled in both roles.

While Rita's arrangement might not work in your situation, the principles of creating role clarity, expectations, and boundaries and building up skills to improve balance can apply in any work situation.

MAKING YOUR ROLES EXTRAORDINARY

Now that you have identified and evaluated your most important roles, how do you transform them into something that will guide you and help you make better decisions about where you invest your attention and energy every day?

The key is to determine your vision of success in each role. You can accomplish this by doing two things:

- Anchor your purpose and passion in a Q2 Role title.
- Craft a Q2 Role Statement for each role.

These two techniques are deeply rooted in brain science. They will help capture your imagination and motivation, so that when you have to make difficult decisions throughout your day, you have these solid mental and emotional foundations to guide your choices, so that you can stay in Q2.

ANCHOR YOUR PURPOSE AND PASSION IN A Q2 ROLE TITLE

When it comes to creating a satisfactory life, passion matters ... a lot.

Daniel Pink, bestselling author of the book *Drive: The Surprising Truth About What Motivates Us,* writes:

> The science shows that the secret to high performance isn't our biological drive or our reward-and-punishment drive, but our third drive—our deep-seated desire to direct our own lives, to extend and expand our abilities, and to make a contribution.[2]

Other research has found that a clear and compelling purpose can reduce stress, improve job performance, increase energy, and keep people from burning out.[3]

A simple technique to capture that spirit and motivation in your roles is to think deeply about your passion and purpose you see and feel in the role. Visualize this clearly in your mind with images of the individuals who are part of your role. What is the contribution you want to make as a mother? Or a supervisor? Or a friend? It is human nature to want to make a contribution—to feel accomplished. What does a vision of success look like to you? What moves both your head and heart?

As you think more deeply about your purpose in a role, you will feel emotion bubble up, and you will try to get your arms around what you are feeling. You will realize how important it is to evoke these feelings, yet you know that they get lost in the day-to-day pressures and chaos.

A great way to bottle this energy is to create an anchor by re-considering the title of your role. What are you feeling? When you think of your role as father, what does that bring up for you? Do you feel accomplishment in that role as being a mentor, a guide, or even a dad? In your role as a manager at work, do you feel in your gut that your greatest contribution in the midst of a busy day might be as a coach, an innovative leader, or a people developer? Do these titles provide you more energy when you think of them? Do they motivate you to make better decisions every day to achieve excellence in that role? If so, retitle your role to capture that feeling.

Here's how Kiva might retitle her roles

Instead of	She might use this
Project Manager	Project Leader
Friend	Lasting Friend
Housemate	Supporter
Photographer	Visual Artist
Daughter	Encourager

The point here is not that these be meaningful or impressive to anyone else, but that they have motivational meaning to you. So be as creative as you'd like! If there is a word, a combination of words, or even an abbreviation that has meaning and evokes a stronger purpose in you, go ahead and use it. If the title you already have creates the passion you need, then stick with that one. The point is to have a title that generates the passion and purpose that will drive you to fight to achieve your greatest contribution in each of your roles.

Take a few minutes and think broadly and deeply about one of your roles. Really go to town on what a vision of success could look and feel like. Capture it in the title of that role. If you like it, then keep going with your other roles.

CRAFT A Q2 ROLE STATEMENT FOR EACH ROLE

Even more powerful than a Q2 Role title is the more specific vision of what success in that role looks like to you, including the kind of activities you will be doing to create that success. That is captured in a Q2 Role Statement. Because of the way the brain works, the more specific and descriptive you can be, particularly about the process of achieving your vision, the more likely you are to be motivated to do the things that will help you accomplish it.[4]

Essentially, this means that, for each role, you craft a brief statement that articulates the outcomes you are after and the essential activities or methods that will help you achieve them. You are not looking for a specific measurable output here (like a goal). That will come later. Rather, you are looking for a combination of outcomes and activities that will guide your goals, plans, and decisions later on.

Here's a formula that can be helpful:

As	I will	By
Role Title	Extraordinary Outcomes	Activities

For example, in Jaivon's role as husband, which he changed to Kalisha's Best Friend, he might say:

As	I will	By
Kalisha's Best Friend	Create an enduring relationship of trust, safety, and mutual discovery	Actively sharing her goals and dreams, spending quality time together, and earning her complete confidence in all my activities and interactions with others.

This statement represents a lot of investment of thought and energy out of the prefrontal-cortex Thinking Brain. It is conscious and intentional. Because Jaivon has taken the time to meaningfully and clearly define what success looks like in this role, it will result in a lot of different decisions about how he invests his time, attention, and energy every day.

If Jaivon consistently and consciously thinks about this statement (which is not always easy, but definitely doable) as part of his Weekly and Daily Q2 Planning (*see* Choice 3), he will likely achieve the "enduring relationship of trust, safety and mutual discovery" he wants, adding great value to both his and Kalisha's lives.

Here's another example from Kiva:

As	I will	By
A Project Leader	Build a team that pushes the boundaries of what is possible	Looking for places where clear processes and better technologies can unleash the creativity of our team to do more compelling work for our clients.

Again, it is clear that Kiva has put some solid thinking into this statement. The final version was not likely created in five minutes of brainstorming. However, we do find it surprising how often people can quickly come up with a Q2 Role Statement that really captures the essence of what they would like to achieve. This happens because these statements come from what people know best— their lives!

Even these versions are not final. Your most important current roles are dynamic; they are constantly changing. A parent who has a three-year-old son now may craft a very different role statement when that son is a teenager or grows to become a parent himself.

These role statements do not go on a shelf or in the back of a book, filed away to be reviewed once a year. A Q2 Role Statement is a living, breathing document of your life today. It captures what is important to you now and what accomplishment looks like to you now. The more you engage with this statement, get excited by it, tweak it, and make it real, the more your brain will have the clarity and anchors to make the right decisions to get the most important things done every day.

All it takes is some reflective time where you can quiet your Reactive Brain, turn on your Thinking Brain, and ask yourself what matters most in each of these few, most important roles in your life today. As you take this contemplative time, be sensitive to the intuitive thoughts and feelings and potential insights you will have about each role.

MAKE SURE THESE Q2 ROLE STATEMENTS ARE TRULY YOUR OWN

Taking the time to craft these statements allows you to get out in the open the expectations you probably already have about yourself but that have just been lurking beneath the surface. It also allows you to confront expectations that may not be yours and, upon examination, really don't belong in your life at all. Remember, this is not about someone else's definition of *extraordinary*. It's about yours. Your Q2 Role Statement should come from the unique context and realities of your own life.

When Michaela took the time to think about her roles, she came to her role as a mom. As she began to answer the question, "What does an extraordinary mom look like?" she could feel her sense of stress and guilt rising. This had always been an area of frustration for her. She grew up in a family where her mom was at home all the time and seemed to do everything right. She was raised with high expectations, and her mom spent a lot of time helping her kids with homework, attending school plays, taking her children to the park, and so forth. Her mom was a constant and, she felt, a nearly perfect presence in her life. Their home was always clean and everything seemed to be in perfect order.

By contrast, Michaela felt she was doing her best simply to stay afloat—trying to balance her career, her family, and her other responsibilities in the community. She felt her house was a mess most of the time, and that her five-year-old daughter barely knew her. Just last week, when she came home from work, her daughter cried and ran to the door when the nanny left, and it ripped Michaela apart.

As these emotions flooded over her, she almost skipped over this role. But then she said, "Wait a minute! What does extraordinary look like in my circumstances with my daughter and my realities?"

As she thought more deeply, she realized that she was laying over her own life a set of expectations from an entirely different set of circumstances, then beating herself up because she couldn't achieve them.

She realized that her daughter was very important to her, and that maybe a clean house wasn't that big a priority. She also realized that maybe there were some other choices she could make that would affect how she spent her time with her daughter before and after work, as well as on the weekends.

As Michaela let go of the definition of success she had been subconsciously carrying around and began to define what extraordinary looked like for her, she began to feel both relief and hope.

Michaela's experience is not uncommon. Research shows that women's lives are particularly susceptible to a sense of feeling overwhelmed based on the number of roles they have and the totality of their experience in managing them. This effect is called role overload. So it is important not only to look at each role, but at how all the roles fit together.[5] As one woman said, "There's a myth that you can have everything. You can't. But you can have time for the things that are most important to you."[6]

CREATING BALANCE AMONG YOUR ROLES

Creating balance among your roles is especially important in today's technology-permeated, always-on, ever-accessible-for-work lifestyle.

In this kind of world, you have an open portal into your life through the gadgets you carry with you. They allow others to beep you, buzz you—even see you!—and to send emails or texts your way anytime, day or night. The only boundaries that exist are the ones you create for yourself and negotiate with others.

This can be a very dangerous reality when it comes to creating balance in your life. However, these technologies can also be very liberating when you have a clear definition of how the important Q2 Roles in your life fit together.

With the creative nature of knowledge work, your best thinking and ideas may come at five in the morning, and your least productive time may be two in the afternoon. Organizations and individuals who have adapted to this reality are less concerned about face time at the office and more concerned about results. In some organizations we know, it is completely acceptable for someone to leave at two on a Wednesday to go biking in the mountains, because she will be taking part in an international video call from six until ten-thirty that evening at home. This person is still fulfilling her role at work while taking time to fulfill her role to take care of herself. Because she has a clear set of outcomes and expectations she has negotiated with others, she does not feel guilty while biking, neither does she feel put upon when taking the call.

In this case, balance is not really about having an eight-hour workday that you then leave behind when you go home. It's also not like some sort of mechanical scale, where when one side (or role) goes up, the other must go down. Instead, visualize life balance like the motion of a graceful dancer or skilled martial artist performing a routine. In this setting, balance is interactive and constantly in motion. Its shape is different at different times—sometimes fast, sometimes slow, but always centered. The goal in your life is to create a harmonious relationship among all your different roles that gives you a sense of satisfaction and achievement, both in the moment and over time.

Take some time now to draft a role statement for each of your roles. Feel free to use the creative Q2 Role titles you came up with earlier as you do this work for each of your roles. Or you can come up with creative titles now. Sometimes these two things evolve together. In the end, you should have a Q2 Role title and a Q2 Role Statement for each role that both clarifies what your desired outcomes are and motivates you to achieve them.

MAKING YOUR ROLES TANGIBLE: SETTING Q2 GOALS

To increase the probability of achieving your vision of success in your most important current Q2 Roles, you can choose one or more very specific and measurable Q2 Goals for each role.

There are a lot of structures out there for setting goals. You've probably heard of SMART goals (Specific, Measurable, Achievable, Relevant, and Time-Bound) or something similar.

Our experience in working with people and organizations around the world who achieve goals suggests that the best way to format your Q2 Goals is to use the following simple formula:

From X to Y by When

What this means is that you want to make a change in a specific outcome (the X and the Y) by a certain date (the when).

Here are some examples:

- Reduce my weight from 230 pounds to 180 pounds by June 17.
- Increase sales from £1 million to £1.8 million by December 31.
- Increase contact with my aging father from zero to three times per week.
- Increase my personal savings rate from 15 percent to 20 percent of my income by January 1.

Some goals may be harder to measure, like improving the feeling you have in a relationship or your sense of satisfaction in your career. But even in these circumstances, you can attach a subjective scale (say, from 1 to 10) and use it to assess where you are and measure your progress. For example:

- Raise the level of trust my spouse has in me from a 5 to an 8 by March 31.

- Increase my own sense of job satisfaction from a 7 to a 9 by May 17.
- Increase my confidence in public speaking from a 2 to a 5 by February 1.

In some cases, goals could be measured simply by an honest look-yourself-in-the-mirror assessment of where you are at various times. Other goals, like increasing the trust your spouse has in you, could be measured by asking your spouse!

In any case, the more specific and measurable your goals are, the more your brain engages with them and the easier they are to achieve.

Once you have set your goals, you can identify the specific activities that will help you achieve them (like exercise and diet for the weight goal, or outbound calls for the sales goal). Then you can act on them consistently each week, which we will talk about in the next chapter. The key is to not pick too many goals and to make sure they tie strongly to the vision and passion that comes from your Q2 Role Statements.

Dr. Heidi Halvorson, one of the preeminent researchers in the field of goal achievement, says:

> We often are reluctant to set very meaningful, difficult goals for ourselves. But well over a thousand studies show that when people set difficult and specific goals for themselves, they are vastly more successful and vastly more satisfied and happy with their lives than they are when they just say, "Well, I'm gonna do my best." [7]

Because setting Q2 Goals represents focusing your attention and energy on some things and away from other things, make sure you choose your goals carefully, in the same mindful and conscious way you crafted your Q2 Role Statements. That way you can be sure the outcome will truly be worth the effort, in the midst of everything else you have going on.

THE POWER OF PURPOSE

In this chapter, we've talked about the importance of creating Q2 Roles and Goals to help you guide your decisions throughout the day. These structures help your brain as you choose where to focus your attention and energy each day to create the highest value.

In addition to connecting to the motivational centers of our brains, clarifying our roles and goals taps into the deepest purposes we have in our lives. Our roles embrace our most significant relationships, our most profound joys, and our highest contributions and aspirations. They tap into our hearts and our spirits. As Daniel Pink states:

> In business, we tend to obsess over the how—as in "Here's how to do it." Yet we rarely discuss the why—as in "Here's why we're doing it." But it's often difficult to do something exceptionally well if we don't know the reasons we're doing it in the first place.[8]

The Q2 time you take to think deeply about your Q2 Roles and Goals will help you tap into these deeper wells of motivation and high performance.

SIMPLE WAYS TO GET STARTED

You can begin applying the principles and practices of Choice 2: Go for Extraordinary, Don't Settle for Ordinary by taking any of the following simple actions. Pick the ones that work best for you.

- Gain some clarity by identifying your most important roles and putting them on a Life Wheel.
- Complete the spidergram exercise to evaluate where you stand in relation to your roles. Celebrate where you are successful!
- Pick an important role where you may need some feedback, and talk to the appropriate person.
- Pick one role and quickly write out a draft Q2 Role Statement. Don't try to make it perfect. Come back to it a day or two later and see if it still makes sense. Improve the statement from there.
- Pick one goal you feel is important and put it into the From X to Y by When formula.

TO SUM UP

- Extraordinary productivity means going to bed each day feeling satisfied and accomplished.
- Identifying the few most important roles we play in our lives right now gives a framework for balance, motivation, and fulfillment.
- Anchoring our motivation in Q2 Role titles and Q2 Role Statements strengthens our ability to make good decisions about where we spend our time and energy each day.
- Honest assessment of our role performance can help us make our roles more extraordinary.
- Setting specific Q2 Goals helps direct our brains in the most productive ways.

ATTENTION
MANAGEMENT

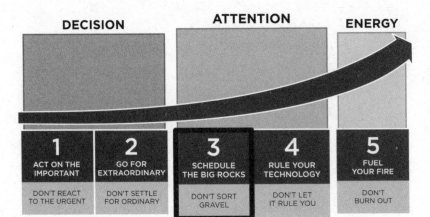

DECISION   ATTENTION   ENERGY

1	2	3	4	5
ACT ON THE IMPORTANT	GO FOR EXTRAORDINARY	SCHEDULE THE BIG ROCKS	RULE YOUR TECHNOLOGY	FUEL YOUR FIRE
DON'T REACT TO THE URGENT	DON'T SETTLE FOR ORDINARY	DON'T SORT GRAVEL	DON'T LET IT RULE YOU	DON'T BURN OUT

SCHEDULE THE BIG ROCKS, DON'T SORT GRAVEL

What's in short supply is human attention. . . . Understanding and managing attention is now the single most important determinant of business success.

—Thomas Davenport and John C. Beck[1]

There is a big difference between thinking about what is important and actually accomplishing it. If we don't have robust planning disciplines and processes in place to execute what is important, then our Q2 Role Statements and Q2 Goals are merely wishful thinking.

Choices 1 and 2 are about making good decisions about where to spend our attention and energy. Choices 3 and 4 are about how we keep our attention focused and intentional to ensure we feel accomplished at the end of every day.

THE BIG ROCKS AND THE GRAVEL

In this comparison, the Big Rocks represent the important Q2 priorities in our lives—time spent on key relationships and responsibilities, important projects, critical meetings, and so forth. These are the activities that come from our Q2 Role Statements and Q2 Goals. These activities are in contrast to gravel, which represents all the little things that fill up our lives—email, phone calls, laundry, less important priorities, and so on. These things take time and attention away from the Big Rocks.

So if the bucket in the picture represents your life, which image makes you feel more accomplished?

If you chose the one on the left, you may be in trouble, because you are putting all the little things in first, then trying to fit in the important things.

In today's world, with its endless onslaught of gravel, this approach simply doesn't work. Instead of small piles of gravel, it seems as though we start each day faced with a long line of dump trucks, all backed up and ready to unload mountains of gravel into our lives.

If you picked the one on the right, you are well on your way to mastering the key concept in Choice 3, which is that you will be more productive if you put all the important things in first, then let some of the inevitable gravel fill in around them.

The key shift in thinking for Choice 3 is to realize that you can never get ahead by just sorting through the gravel faster. It's a losing battle. Instead, you must decide what is most important (Choices 1 and 2), then schedule your weeks and days in such a way that you can focus your precious attention and energy on those things first (Choice 3).

To make this work, you need to become intentional about letting go of a lot of the little things. It's okay! In fact, many of those things are self-imposed Q3s that keep you from getting more fully into Q2. You can consciously choose to leave some of the gravel outside the jar, just as you see in the picture.

In the old mindset of time management, the message was this: Everyone has the same amount of time, but some people can cram more in the spaces than others. They must be the most productive.

In today's environment, the key to true productivity is not to get more things done, but to get the right things done—the important things—with the highest quality you can achieve. It's not about doing more with less, but doing more *about* less. It's about concentrating more of your very best attention and energy on those few priorities that really matter and getting them done in the midst of the inevitable gravel in our lives.

Throughout the rest of this chapter, you will learn the critical principles and processes of Q2 Planning—the kind of planning that gets the important things done.

A CRITICAL PRE-PLANNING TOOL:
THE MASTER TASK LIST

Before we dive into the Q2 Planning process itself, we need to spend a little time on a vital tool that supports the process: the Master Task List.

Do you have a task list already? Do you have two or more? Or, like many people, do you jot down important tasks on whatever happens to be available at the time, stuff it in your bag or purse, and hope you find it later? (Be honest!) When you're looking for important information on redundant lists or on scraps of paper that have fluttered down under your desk, which quadrant are you in?

In the twenty-first century, the Master Task List is probably one of the most vital tools we can use to keep our attention focused on Q2. Used properly, a Master Task List can act as another filter to discern and organize the incoming to ensure we are acting on our most important priorities.

The purpose of a Master Task List is to keep things in a single trustworthy tracking system so that you can get them out of your brain and stop worrying about them. Then, when you do your Q2 Planning, you can confidently refer to your Master Task List, knowing that the important things you need to think about are there.

The basic rule for using a Master Task List is this: When something comes up that you might need to do, it goes either *on the floor or on the list,* but not in your head. This means you use your discernment skills right away and decide what to do with it, but don't leave it floating in your consciousness, taking up valuable working memory. The Time Matrix helps you make these decisions. Specifically:

- **Q3s and Q4s go on the floor.** By definition, Q3s and Q4s are not important. Thus, if something is a Q3 or a Q4 and you can safely get rid of it, then toss it *on the floor,* meaning that you have successfully discerned and dismissed some incoming gravel that would otherwise be filling your day. Give yourself a high-five so that your brain knows you've done the right thing and move on.
- **Q2s and Q1s go on the list.** If it is a Q2 or a necessary Q1, then put it on the list. That way, you record your choice to spend time and attention on it later, and can focus on getting your work done, rather than keeping the task floating in your head. Once a task is written down, you have already raised the probability of accomplishing it and have put your mind at peace, allowing you to focus your attention on more important things.

Later, when you pull out your list to do your planning, keep in mind that, due to changing circumstances, what may have been important when you wrote it down may not be important now, so don't be bound by what you put on the list. Feel free to toss something on the floor if it is no longer important.

If you are wondering whether something goes on the floor or on the list, you can ask yourself questions like:

- Am I writing down a Q3?
- Am I volunteering to take care of someone else's responsibility, when I don't really have to?
- Am I writing down a Q1 for the fifth time because I'm not finding a way to prevent it from happening? (In that case, write down another Q2 task to prevent that Q1 in the future.)

- Am I writing down something that should be delegated to someone else? (In that case, you might change the task to delegate that item.)

The Master Task List allows you to figuratively pull up the Time Matrix in the moment of choice, and use your discernment to decide if you should be acting on this task at all. If the answer is *no*, then it goes on the floor. If the answer is *yes*, then it goes on the list.

What you should not do is put everything on the list just to get it out of your head. This just turns your list into a gravel collector. Anything you can keep off your list is a decision well made, and represents a positive choice to focus more attention on the Big Rocks—your Q2 Roles and Goals.

If you are not sure whether something is important or will require some additional time to accurately discern, then put it on the list, but don't use this as an excuse for laziness in filtering out things that shouldn't be there.

Without a Master Task List, you are more prone to have sleepless nights, tossing and turning as all the things you need to do and haven't written down run through your mind like a broken record. You also feel the pressure of knowing that tomorrow a whole new slew of decisions and demands are coming your way, and that you have nowhere to put them. Keeping these things in your head instead of on a list reduces the amount of working memory you have in your brain to focus on other important things.

Now that we have a basic handle on the Master Task List, let's see how it plays out in our Q2 Planning.

Q2 PLANNING AND THE 30/10 PROMISE

We want to make you a promise: If you spend thirty minutes each week and ten minutes each day in Q2 Planning, you will dramatically increase your ability to be and feel accomplished at the end of every day. It is a process that will transform the way you approach every other hour you spend. According to Dr. Heidi Halvorson, a leading researcher on goals and achievement:

> Planning turns out to be one of the single most effective strategies you can use in order to reach any goal. When people engage in the right kind of planning, their success rates go up on average between 200 percent to 300 percent.[2]

Q2 Planning is a process where you take some time to quiet your mind and work from the Thinking Brain to consciously and intentionally load the Big Rocks into your weeks and days *first*, to make sure they get accomplished.

Why does it take thirty minutes each week? Because it takes a few minutes to get into that zone. Otherwise, you will be working from your Reactive Brain, which will lead you to schedule urgencies, rather than planning from your Q2 Thinking Brain, which allows you to organize around that which is most important.

When you take some time to reduce the noise, get centered, and plan from a more thoughtful state, you will have an entirely different experience when you ask yourself, *What is most important?* The answers you get will be clearer and more accurate.

In the words of Buddhist monk and philosopher in meditation and neuroscience, Tenzin Priyadarshi:

If there is no stillness, there is no silence. If there is no silence, there is no insight. If there is no insight, there is no clarity.[3]

You don't need to reach Nirvana to practice Q2 Planning, but if you approach the process thoughtfully, you will gain additional insight and clarity, and the Big Rocks in your life won't get buried by the gravel.

Q2 TIME ZONES

One high-value practice that sets you up for effective Weekly and Daily Q2 Planning is to create Q2 Time Zones. These are proactively scheduled blocks of time that help you protect your Q2 priorities.

The value of Time Zones is that you can plan them in advance, either as repeating activities or one-time events, so that when you come to a new week, there is already some Q2 time there waiting for you.

Here are some examples:

- Kiva wants to exercise in the morning, so she may block out time from six-thirty to seven-thirty each morning to go to her living room and do her yoga program. She can set this up as a repeating event in her electronic calendar. According to one study, the simple act of scheduling a specific time and place to exercise increased success rates from 32 percent to 91 percent in terms of actual follow-through on a commitment to exercise.[4]

- If Jaivon's best thinking time is in the morning, he might block out an hour or two for that each day, or on certain days during the week. Then he might set aside some afternoon time for meetings so they have a place to go and it won't interfere with his morning thinking time.

- If Sherry wants to make sure she invests time with her husband each week, she could block out Friday nights as a repeating date night.
- Brad, an executive with a busy and often unpredictable travel schedule, could look ahead several months and lay out time that is available for travel and block out other times, like vacation, that would be off limits, except in the direst of circumstances.

Here's what Jaivon's week might look like once he has set up some repeating Q2 Time Zones:

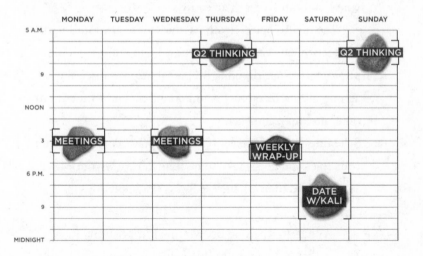

WEEKLY Q2 PLANNING

Once you have your Master Task List and your Q2 Time Zones established, you are ready to plan your week. Find a quiet place and take at least thirty minutes *before* your week starts to:

1. **Review Your Roles and Goals.** Take some time to consciously connect with the vision for your life that you captured in your Q2 Role Statements and Q2 Goals. Don't skimp on this step. It will rekindle your deepest passion and highest motivations. If you do not review this regularly, you can get pulled into the busyness of your days, and that vision will fade away into the depths of your memory as your brain fights to survive the onslaught of immediately pressing demands. So make sure they are in a format and in a place where you can access them easily.

    The neurological truth is that to be extraordinarily productive, our vision must literally be top of mind—in the prefrontal-cortex Thinking Brain that helps us discern what, among all the incoming, is important enough to merit our time, attention, and energy.

2. **Schedule the Big Rocks.** Once you have connected with your roles and goals, take some time to review your Master Task List and then ask the Big Rocks Question:

    > What are the one or two most important
    > things I can do in this role this week?

    As you carefully consider each of your life's roles and ask this question, the answers will come to your gut as well as to your mind. There may be some that are pretty obvious, like the big project that is due this week. Some may be less obvious and require greater sensitivity to discern, like something you need to do in a key relationship, or some preparation you could make to improve the results of a big meeting scheduled later in the week.

All of the things going on in your life are represented somewhere in your brain. However, if you never take time to listen to the more subtle connections and feelings you may have about these things, you can easily miss some of the highest-return investments of your time and attention in the upcoming week.

Note that some of these activities may never have been on your Master Task List to begin with. Usually, these subtle directions do not come at you strongly enough during the day to cut through the noise and busyness. However, when you are quiet and thoughtfully considering your Q2 Roles and Goals, you can gain tremendous insight as to where you should focus your time, attention, and energy for the greatest return. When these insights come to you, and if they are something you need to act on, you can put these on your Master Task List as well.

When you are finally clear as to the most important activities for this week, schedule these Big Rocks into your calendar!

There is great value in actually *scheduling* an appointment to do something, rather than simply putting it on a general task list for the day. Too often daily task lists become daily wish lists, and they end up simply floating from day to day with little progress.

Scheduling a specific time and place to do something represents a higher-level commitment, and dramatically increases the likelihood that you will do it. This is because increased specificity cues your brain to take action when that time arrives. It also helps you manage your time against Q3 distractions, which can occur when somebody pops into your office because your calendar seems free.

When you are planning your week, put something on a daily task list only as a last resort—if you really aren't sure when, or if, it will be done. If you want to do something, in almost every case it is better to schedule it in as a specific appointment during the day.

Finally, when it comes to Big Rocks, you should only pick the top one or two most important things for each role. There is only so much you can do, so set the bar high and pick the ones that will really make a difference. This increases the likelihood that they will actually be accomplished in the realities of the busy week ahead.

3. **Organize the Rest.** With the Big Rocks securely in place, you can calendar other important things that need to be done—even some of the gravel—things that aren't critical, but need to be taken care of, like the laundry!

These three steps to Weekly Q2 Planning will ensure that your week looks like the productive bucket, rather than the unproductive bucket.

Here's how a typical gravel-filled week might have looked for Kiva:

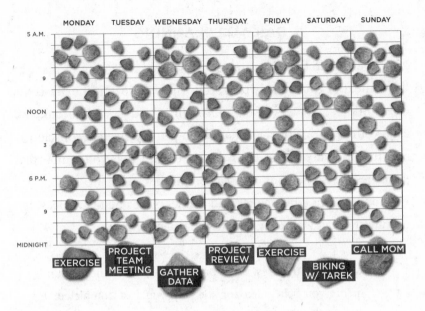

If Kiva had practiced some Q2 Planning, she might have ended her week looking more like this:

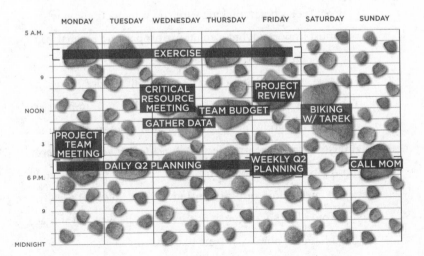

DAILY Q2 PLANNING

Now, we realize that life rarely, if ever, goes according to plan. In the context of your weekly plan, you will need to adjust daily as the week unfolds. Gravel will be pouring in, Q1 crises will occur, and even your Q2 priorities can change. So you will need to consciously and intentionally adjust each day to ensure that your important priorities get carried out, one way or another.

To plan your coming day, find a quiet place and take at least ten minutes to review the day you just completed, and:

1. **Close Out the Day.** Look back at your tasks and appointments you scheduled for the day you just completed. Is everything done? If not, then reschedule the unfinished items at some other time on your calendar, delete them if they are no longer important, or leave them on your Master Task List with any adjustments that are necessary to due dates or similar details. The idea is to be accountable to yourself for each day, making sure you were focused on what was most important, but also taking proper care of what you may have moved or rescheduled in the process.

   Also, you'll want to do what we call *capture the gold.* Throughout the day, there were probably some important bits of information, new tasks, insights, or ideas that came along the way. Capturing the gold means that you make sure those bits of information end up in the right place for you to use later (More on this coming up in Choice 4.) Ideally, you would have done much of this along the way, but if that didn't happen, now is the time to do it.

2. **Identify the Few "Must-Dos."** Ask yourself, "What are the few must-dos I want to achieve in the coming day?" A *must-do* is something so important that you probably wouldn't end your day without getting it done. Usually, you're just recommitting to your Big Rocks, but you might have to deal with some Q1s that have come up.

3. **Organize the Rest.** Organize everything else around your must-dos.

These three steps can be done at the end of the day you just completed or on the morning of the next day.

People who do these three steps at the end of the day tend to do so because they feel they are better prepared to relax for the rest of the evening. They know that everything is taken care of and in the right place. They can sleep better because they don't have a bunch of loose ends and unfinished business floating around in their heads.

People who do these steps the next morning tend to do so because, at the end of the day, their thinking may not be as clear as it is in the morning, after a good night's sleep.

Some people actually split the steps and do step 1 (close out the day) in the evening, but do steps 2 and 3 in the morning when their minds are clearer and they can be more sensitive to insights that may come when they think through what is most important.

However you choose do it, the key is to pick an approach that allows you to have a few moments in a Q2 mindset before the activity of the new day begins. Otherwise, you'll simply be diving headfirst into the flow of incoming gravel, hoping you will find some time to come up for air and get some of the more important things done. When it comes to being highly productive, this is not an effective approach.

Q2 PLANNING: THINKING IN THE SHOWER

When do your most creative ideas come? Early in the morning? After a good night's sleep? In the shower? Have there been times in your life where your goals and priorities seemed to be crystal clear and everything seemed to be in the right place?

Our guess is that you have had a number of times when you felt this way, only to have these moments fade quickly beneath the onslaught of your busy days.

Our question is: Why can't you have these moments more often?

Our position is that, with regular Q2 Planning, not only can you have such moments of clarity and perspective more often, but they can actually become a hallmark of the way you live your days.

As we learned in Choice 1, our brain rewires itself based on how we use it. If we develop a weekly and daily habit of connecting with our highest priorities and organizing our lives around those things, Q2 starts to become our normal way of thinking. We start to carry a centered Q2 mindset with us throughout each day. This enables us to respond more quickly and calmly to unanticipated changes in our schedule. Instead of stressing out, we handle these changes with more confidence and ease because we are coming from a sense of organization and a practiced Q2 perspective.

Someone asked a Zen master how he maintained his deep sense of peace throughout the pressures of the day. He replied, "I never leave my place of meditation."[5]

When we take the time each week and day to connect with

our deeper priorities, we can carry that solid sense of perspective with us throughout the day. We become the calm in the midst of the storm—able to rise above the torrent of gravel that threatens to bury our most important priorities.

SIMPLE WAYS TO GET STARTED

You can begin applying the principles and practices of Choice 3: Schedule the Big Rocks, Don't Sort Gravel by taking any of the following simple actions. Pick the ones that work best for you.

- Set up a Master Task List and practice the on-the-floor-or-on-the-list rule three times today. Give yourself a high-five when you successfully throw something on the floor!
- Review the past few weeks in your mind. Identify one or two repeating patterns that could be set up and better managed as Q2 Time Zones.
- Decide when and where you will do your Weekly and Daily Q2 Planning. Schedule these as recurring Q2 Time Zones on your calendar.

TO SUM UP

- You can never get ahead by just sorting through the gravel faster. Decide what is most important and get those activities in the bucket before the week begins.
- When a task comes up that you might need to do, it goes either on the floor or on the list, but not in your head!
- Q2 Time Zones are proactively scheduled blocks of time that help you protect your recurring Q2 priorities.
- The three steps for Weekly Q2 Planning are: (1) Review your Roles and Goals, (2) Schedule the Big Rocks, and (3) Organize the Rest. The three steps for Daily Q2 Planning are: (1) Close Out the Day, (2) Identify the Few "Must-Dos," and (3) Organize the Rest.
- The 30/10 Promise will transform the time you spend everywhere else and dramatically increase your ability to feel accomplished at the end of every day.

ATTENTION MANAGEMENT

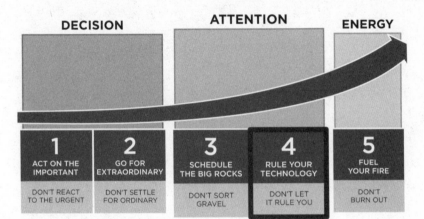

DECISION		ATTENTION		ENERGY
1 ACT ON THE IMPORTANT	**2** GO FOR EXTRAORDINARY	**3** SCHEDULE THE BIG ROCKS	**4** RULE YOUR TECHNOLOGY	**5** FUEL YOUR FIRE
DON'T REACT TO THE URGENT	DON'T SETTLE FOR ORDINARY	DON'T SORT GRAVEL	DON'T LET IT RULE YOU	DON'T BURN OUT

RULE YOUR TECHNOLOGY, DON'T LET IT RULE YOU

In the midst of chaos, there is also opportunity.

—Sun Tzu, *The Art of War*

In 1967, futurist Herman Kahn envisioned a scenario in which, by the year 2000, one of our cultural challenges would be the impact of increased leisure time brought on by productivity technologies. He thought most people could be working about thirty hours per week and have thirteen weeks of vacation.[1] (If only!) He wrote,

> . . . the "normal" worker could spend less than 50 percent of his days on his vocation [career] . . . less than 50 percent of his days on his avocation [hobbies or other interests] . . . and then still have one or two days off a week for just relaxing. In other words, it would be possible to pursue an avocation as intensely as a vocation and still have a good deal of time for [other] pursuits.[2]

In the nearly four decades since Kahn wrote those words, we have invented countless productivity technologies from sticky notes to personal computers, from email to video conferencing, the Internet, the cell phone, text messaging, wireless networking, wearable devices that tell us where we are and where to go, eBooks, HDTV, even gloves that produce music![3] The list goes on and on.

But have these technologies made you more productive? Do you feel anything close to the kind of freedom and flexibility that was described by Herman Kahn? Or do you feel more like a slave to the dings and pings of your smartphone, email, or tablet?

TECHNOLOGY: YOUR DRUG OF CHOICE?

In Choice 1: Act on the Important, Don't React to the Urgent, we talked about the process of becoming addicted to urgency. The truth is that technology can amp up the addictive power of urgency tenfold. It's like smoking crack cocaine, which is both more immediately stimulating and more addictive than cocaine in a powdered form. It is also significantly more dangerous!

Our current technologies can provide such immediate responsiveness to our actions that we can be caught up in responding to texts and tweets, thinking we are being productive, when in fact we are really only being distracted.

Of greater concern, we may be missing the really important things like building strong relationships, collaborating on important problems, or doing some thoughtful and focused work. Because these things are not so clickable, they become less stimulating to our brains than the sounds on our smartphones. But in the end, these things are far more important.

Recently we witnessed a family attending a ballet performance where one of their children was performing. The family was seated near the back, and of the four people in the row, three of them were on their devices playing games—the father and two of the children. Only the mother was looking up at the stage. When the lights came down for the performance to begin, the three people on their devices simultaneously lowered the brightness of their screens and kept going, heads down, faces aglow. It wasn't until someone in the row behind them asked them to turn their devices off that they awkwardly looked up and began to watch the performance.

As Dr. Ed Hallowell, a specialist in attention deficit disorder, recently told us:

> We've created a new addiction. It's the addiction to technology. . . . And so you find people, literally, compulsively reaching for their email like it was a package of cigarettes.[4]

As Catherine Steiner-Adair, a researcher on the effects of technology in family life, stated:

> I am always struck by the one eternal and incontrovertible truth about families: children need their parents' time and attention. . . . But this reality can be so easily lost when we are lured away by the siren call of the virtual world.[5]

Sometimes we hear, "Young people are the ones glued to their technology!" Well, yes, they grew up with technology in their hands. But let's look at our roles as adults. Research shows that young children often feel lonely and depressed because they are competing with smartphones and tablets for their parents' love.[6]

One mid-level manager told us the story of her and her husband's use of technology around their four-year-old child. They felt that they needed to change their behavior, because when they would get home from work, they found themselves getting on their smartphones pretty quick, lost in their own worlds. They decided this was not the best behavior to model for their four-year-old, and they realized life was going by way too fast and that their daughter would not be a baby for long.

So they created a plan, knowing the addiction would be hard to break. They put a basket by the front door and agreed that when they got home, they would put their smartphones in the basket. The basket provided a little accountability system, because both parents' smartphones were visible and would be noticed if removed.

A few days into this new behavior, the parents went to pick up their smartphones in the morning as they walked out the door. What they found next was amazing. In the basket along with their phones was their daughter's little iPod. They had not asked her to do it. In fact, they never even had a discussion with her. But her little mind and heart modeled the behavior of her parents. She set aside her technology to be part of the family!

Although this is an example of positive-behavior modeling, there could be a dark side to this story. Was this child craving her parents' attention? Did she feel as though she were competing with the smartphones for her parents' affection? Did she put her iPod in the basket *hoping* that this would be the way to seal the deal on receiving her parents' love? Whatever the answer, changing technology behavior changed the game for this family, providing deep Q2 attention and energy in the short time between arriving home from work and going back the next day.

Quality attention to relationships is not just for our homes and families. One thirty-something told us that when he and his friends go out to eat, they all put their phones in a basket, and the first one to pick up his or her phone during the meal has to pay for everyone. For them, this is a great way to encourage direct interaction and affirm the relationships they want to have as friends.

WHO'S IN CHARGE HERE?

The first step in making technology your servant and not your master is to come to terms with how you are behaving with your own technology. Think about this through the lens of the Time Matrix. At work and at home, are you using your technology in a Q3 or Q4 kind of way? Are you lured by the urgency of the dings and pings, but responding to things that are ultimately unimportant? Are you lured by the excess of a particular game that is neither urgent nor important, but somehow takes hours of your time, attention, and energy that obviously would be better used elsewhere?

Once you've confronted your own relationship with technologies, you are in a position to use them as powerful tools to help you move into Q2. In the end, technology is not the problem; it is how conscious and deliberate we are about how we use it. Our brains may love the novelty, but by getting very clear as to what is really important to us and using our conscious skills of discernment, we have every chance to use our tools wisely to achieve extraordinary productivity every day.

SWORDLESSNESS AND THE FIRST PRINCIPLE

Sometimes we get caught up in the idea that if we just have the right tool—the right software, the latest gadget, and so on—then all our problems will be solved. But this is wishful thinking. Although we appreciate the time-saving advantages some technologies can offer, if we want to live meaningful and productive lives, we cannot outsource our fundamental human right and ability to make wise choices for ourselves. No external device can replace our own minds.

When we embrace the idea that no tool will automatically save us, we act from what sixteenth-century Japanese sword master Yagyū Munenori called the "first principle," which is to be independent in every possible way, and to keep your presence of mind in all circumstances.[7] It also means that we embrace the ideal of *swordlessness*, which means you can use all tools freely to win the battle.[8] The notion is that when we get stuck on a particular tool, we create an attachment in our mind that keeps us from moving fluidly and responding appropriately to different circumstances as they arise. This is important, because the tools and technologies change all the time, but the first principle of conscious choice does not.

> There is a story of a soldier in battle, tired and worn out, who has lost his sword. As he stumbles across the battlefield, he sees the hilt of another sword sticking out of the ground. Elated, he picks up the sword, only to find that it has been broken and that he holds in his hand only half a sword. Discouraged, he throws the broken sword to the ground and says to himself, "If only I had the Emperor's shining sword of gold and the finest steel, then

I could fight the battle and win!" Giving up hope, the soldier sulks away and leaves the battle.

A few minutes later, another tired figure comes to the same place and picks up the same sword. As he sees the broken blade, he raises it jubilantly to the sky and, with renewed vigor and a shout, returns to the battle. Leading his armies with a broken sword, the Emperor turns the tide to victory.

Why would we use a martial-arts metaphor to talk about technology? Because the battle for our attention is real and, more important, it *feels* like a battle. Dealing with the vast amount of incoming while trying to overcome the allure of our technology is difficult. It takes real effort to defend our most important priorities and give them our finest attention and energy.

In this chapter, we will identify some very practical skills and processes you can use, regardless of your technologies, to stay in Q2. They will take some practice to implement, but they are powerful and will make a significant difference in your results. What gives these skills their power is the underlying Q2 mindset and the first principle of choice. While good technologies can help us in the battle, it is the Q2 mindset that helps us win.

PREPARING FOR THE BATTLE: WHERE'S YOUR STUFF?

The first thing we need to do is to get all our information organized.

If you're like most people, gravel comes at you all day from all directions. Your smartphone takes messages, texts, and tweets. Your email accounts fill up like a clogged sink. You take a phone call and write the message on any piece of paper that's handy. Your workspace is cluttered with letters, documents, and sticky notes. You might take notes on your phone or on your computer or in a notebook or on any available legal pad—or all of these. You tell yourself that someday you're going to get it all organized, but it seems an overwhelming chore. How do you even begin to tackle it all?

Whether it's thousands of emails in your inbox or a pile on your desk, there is actually order in the chaos. You just need the ability to see it.

THE CORE 4

Basically, there are four kinds of information you need to manage—two of them you can act on; the other two are information that you file away for future reference.

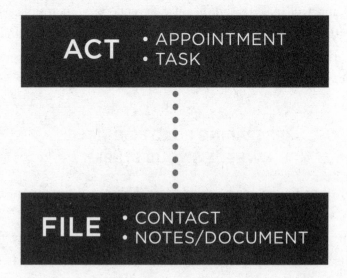

- **Appointments.** Things you need to do at specific times.
- **Tasks.** Things you need to do that are not yet scheduled.
- **Contacts.** Information about people you interact with.
- **Notes/Documents.** Other information you want to keep track of that does not fall into one of the other three categories.

We call these categories the *Core 4*. The first task to bring order to the chaos is to learn to see incoming information in terms of these four categories. The next step is to create a system to manage your important information so you know exactly where and how to access it anywhere, anytime. How you do that will depend on the system you use, but as a guideline, we recommend the *Rule of One.*

This means having one Master Task List, one calendar, one contacts list, and one system for your notes or documents. This can be personalized, as long as you stay true to the principles managing the Core 4. You can design your system to be all paper, all digital, or a combination of both.

A PAPER-BASED SYSTEM

Before the proliferation of so many easy-to-use electronic devices, people who had learned the FranklinCovey time-management approach carried their Master Task List, calendars, contacts, and notes pages all under one cover, in the classic paper-based Franklin Planner. And some people still do. There is no need to apologize for a paper-based system in this age of electronics!

The obvious advantage of this system is it keeps everything in one place. It's portable and it appeals to people who like to write things down and have a more tangible and analog representation of their information. It also doesn't need to be charged.

The disadvantage is that it's not connected to anything, which means you can't just gather information or accept appointments with the click of a button. It also means there is no backup, so if you lose it, you are pretty much doomed.

Our current experience is that because so much of our communication and information comes at us digitally via calls, texts, tweets, and emails, it can take a lot of work to faithfully transpose the Core 4 to paper as the incoming speeds at us. But it can be done.

If you prefer paper, you will be more productive and experience fewer headaches if you keep all your personal notes in one notebook, rather than writing them on whatever piece of paper happens to be around. To be effective with a paper-based system for organizing the Core 4, the cardinal rule is "everything in one place."

A DIGITAL SYSTEM

The other end of the spectrum is keeping all your key information digitally. If you do, the rule to follow there is to have "everything in every place." This means having your Core 4 in a system that allows you to access everything consistently across all your devices, no matter where you are.

For example, you could enter a friend's contact information once and immediately have it accessible from your smartphone, tablet, and laptop or from any other computer with Web access. The information itself would be stored on a server somewhere (the cloud), allowing you to access it anywhere there is a connection to the Internet.

The advantage of this approach is that you can have your key information accessible, regardless of which device you happen to have with you at the time. Because this information is stored as bits instead of pages, it also means you can have essentially infinite storage, with years of history and data available to you at the touch of a button. It also makes it easy to take incoming information that is in digital form and file it quickly. It is generally more secure and provides instant backup so that if you lose a device, all of your key information is still available. Finally, it allows you to use this information more easily as you interact and communicate with others.

The disadvantage of this kind of system is that it is easy to get buried under the gravel of the digital incoming. If you don't stay conscious and intentional, these systems can actually accelerate the unstoppable flow of information that can bury you alive. You end up creating a digital wasteland of clutter that suffocates you, rather than helping you stay in Q2.

If you are going to be extraordinarily productive, you need to carefully think about your gadgetry and the Core 4 to make sure you create an elegant system that doesn't inadvertently create redundancy. If at all possible, make sure each one of the Core 4 has a single system that syncs across all of your devices. Purchase any technology you'd like; just be vigilant.

Do not, for example, mindlessly start entering tasks into a renegade task list on your smartphone (just because it's there) if your Master Task List is on your computer. Rather, find an app that syncs the information on both of your devices so that you can enter it once and have it seamlessly appear in both places. There are a number of applications that do this. Just find one you like, and be disciplined about keeping all of your tasks in that system. Pretty soon, it will become second nature. The same principle applies to each of the Core 4.

Consider Martin, a salesperson who has a smartphone, tablet, and laptop. He subscribes to a cloud-based file-sharing service that allows him to keep his critical notes and documents accessible from all of his devices. This service has full-function apps that run on all of his devices so that if he changes a document on one device, the revised version immediately goes to the cloud and is accessible on every device. His calendar and contacts are also stored in the cloud via a separate service so that he can see and update them from any device. He uses a separate task-list service that also has apps for all of his devices. This is where he keeps his Master Task List. So with three carefully chosen software services, he can follow the principle of "everything in every place" for his Core 4.

To help him focus on Q2, Martin categorizes his appointments, tasks, and notes by roles. This allows him to clearly associate his activities and notes with what is important to him. Since Martin is a salesperson and manages his work contacts aggressively, he has two categories: work and personal.

Now, we know that not everyone has the independence Martin has to choose services. You should become familiar with your corporate IT policies as you design your system. You might be required to use a corporate platform like Microsoft Exchange, Google, or some other software. In some cases, your corporate IT policies may make it easy to sync the information in these systems across all your devices. In other cases, you may be facing a litany of firewalls, security policies, and so forth that may limit your ability to stay in sync using these systems. Many folks are not even allowed to access their work systems outside the office. We also hear a lot of people say, "I don't want to mix my personal and work information anyway!"

So now what do you do?

If you have access to your corporate system twenty-four hours a day but are worried about commingling work and personal information, here are some options.

- Some systems allow you to mark personal data (like tasks and appointments) private so that nobody but you can see the details on a shared calendar. That way, you can still schedule time to visit the doctor or clean the garage, and everyone else will simply see that time zone as private.
- If you are uncomfortable doing that, you might decide to have two very distinct sets of Core 4—one personal and one work. You are still following the Rule of One, because each of your work Core 4 will be in one system and each of your personal Core 4 will be in one system. However, there is a big rule to follow if you separate work and personal this way: Never, ever can those two systems commingle! Stick to the conventions you set up. If you become complacent and put a personal task (buy the tickets) on your work task list because it is handy, it will leave your mind and, just when you are putting your feet up to relax, you will find yourself in big trouble because you missed your opportunity to buy the tickets and are now out of luck!
- The approach of two independent sets of Core 4 can solve the access problem as well. If you have no access to or authentication for your tablet and smartphone on your work system, then you can comfortably keep your personal and work Core 4 separate, knowing (again) that never should these two systems meet.

To build your personal system, there are a number of cloud-based services that can be used to manage each, or even several, of the different elements of your Core 4. You can find them simply by going to the app store for whatever devices you use and searching for items like tasks or notes. Some of these services come on your devices already and are designed to sync with other devices. The key is to be conscious about them and to carefully select the best services that allow you to have everything in every place.

We also recommend that you look for one provided by a company that has been around for a while so you can be confident that the system supporting your important information will be around in the future.

A BLENDED APPROACH

When managing the Core 4, the ideal is to have one system for each of the Core 4. It does not mean, however, that all four need to be in one paper-based planner or that all four need to be in a digital system. You may choose a blended system, as long as you have one system for each. You may choose to keep your calendar digitally because it easily syncs across devices. You may choose to do the same with your contacts. You might, however, decide to keep your task list and key notes in a paper-based notebook.

It really doesn't matter what you use, as long as it works for you and you follow the principles that keep it organized. Most important, it should increase your ability to focus on Q2.

ASSESSING YOUR CORE 4

Sherry, for example, took some time to figure out where she currently keeps her Core 4. Here's what she found:

- **Appointments.** She keeps her personal appointments on a small paper calendar in her purse and her work appointments on the corporate system. This violates the Rule of One, potentially leading her to double-schedule and miss important upcoming work appointments during her Weekly Q2 Planning, since she usually accesses this system only at work. Sometimes, she writes down important work events on her paper calendar, but because she doesn't like doing all the double entry, both of her calendars end up being incomplete.
- **Tasks.** She keeps these on a paper task list in her planner. This is a good use of the Rule of One, but Sherry finds she is not gaining the advantages of digital task management.
- **Contacts.** She has two groups of contacts. One is the set of numbers she has on her phone, and the other is the corporate contact list on her computer. Because her systems don't sync, however, she often has duplicate or outdated information on her phone for people in her company.
- **Notes/Documents.** She has paper notes in her notepad and her other documents are stored on her computer. She feels good about how this is working for her.

After some thought, Sherry created an integrated system to better help her manage her Core 4. Here's what she did:

- **Appointments.** After talking to her IT department, Sherry found that she could easily set her phone to view both the company's information and her personal information so that she would have a complete view of her calendar wherever she went and would no longer double-schedule herself. She moved her personal calendar to an online service and now has an integrated view with her at all times.

- **Tasks.** She found an online task service with simple apps that allowed her to keep all her tasks digitally and view them in a unified fashion. She still keeps her work and personal tasks in separate categories, but they show up in the same program, so it is a good use of the Rule of One.

- **Contacts.** The same fix that helped her unify her calendars also helped her unify her contacts. Her personal contacts were already on her phone, so she just needed to weed out some duplicates.

- **Notes/Documents.** Because she likes to write down notes on paper and hasn't found an electronic solution she likes, she kept her note system basically the same. Her personal notes are in her notebook and all of her larger electronic documents stay on her computer.

Here's what her system now looks like:

	PAPER	DIGITAL		
		MOBILE PHONE	TABLET	LAPTOP/DESKTOP
APPOINTMENTS		✓		✓
TASKS		✓		✓
CONTACTS		✓		✓
NOTES/ DOCUMENTS	Personal Notes			Large Documents

With just a couple of changes, Sherry has a much more integrated system for managing her Core 4. Using the Rule of One as her guideline, her appointments and tasks now sync between her mobile phone and laptop. Her critical information is always available for all the roles of her life. She doesn't have a tablet, but she has been thinking about getting one for her birthday. When she does, she now knows that with just a few settings, all her information will immediately be there too. The overall key, as organizing expert Julie Morgenstern states, "is to take the time to evaluate what you have and assign each item a single, consistent home."[9]

LAYING OUT YOUR BATTLE PLAN: THE Q2 PROCESS™ MAP

With a solid system to keep your Core 4 organized, you are now ready to use the Q2 Process Map. This map shows how all you've learned so far fits together to help you win the battle in the daily flow of information. It shows how to leverage your technology to keep your attention and energy focused on the important activities in Q2.

Here's the basic version of the Q2 Process Map.

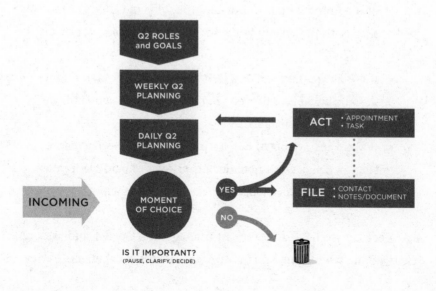

The column in the middle shows how your Q2 Roles and Goals inform your Weekly Q2 Planning and your Daily Q2 Planning, fortifying you in the moment of choice. If that were all there was to it, and life went according to plan, we wouldn't need anything else.

But there's that arrow on the left. This represents the unstoppable flow of incoming information, tasks, appointments, and requests for your time, attention, and energy. It also contains great opportunities and high-return decisions to be made.

The vertical column and the incoming flow come together in the moment of choice, where the battle for our finest attention and energy actually happens. That's where we pause, clarify, and decide to discern what—among all the incoming emails, texts, phone calls, people, and assignments—really matters so that we can defend our Q2 priorities against the things that are less important.

If an incoming item is not important, that means it is a Q3 or Q4, and it follows the lower arrow that points to the trash bin. Since we don't want to spend our valuable time, attention, and energy on this kind of thing, we dismiss it.

If an incoming item is important, then it is in Q1 or Q2 and can be handled with the system you have set up to manage your Core 4!

- If it is an appointment or a task, then you will need to act on it, so it should go either on your calendar as an appointment or into your Master Task List.
- If you can't act on it, but it's information to be referenced later—a contact or a note/document—you should file it into the appropriate location, either electronic or paper.

Because we have a system to manage our Core 4 and we are clear about where our stuff is, we can access it when necessary, and it will automatically be available for our Weekly and Daily Q2 Planning. This ensures that when we are in a reflective, thinking, Q2 Planning mode, we have our most important information organized in a way that will help us get the Big Rocks into our schedules. This self-reinforcing planning and organizing system fuels our ability to discern in each moment of choice so the things that are important do not become casualties in the daily battle for our time, attention, and energy.

THE 3 MASTER MOVES

Now that you understand the essential flow of the basic Q2 Process Map, we'll add three more elements across the bottom to create the complete Q2 Process Map. These are 3 Master Moves that can help you leverage the features of your technology systems to dramatically increase their effectiveness as you deal with the incoming and organize your Core 4.

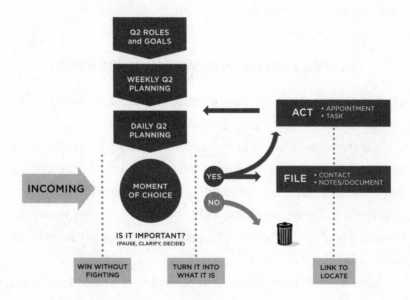

The term *master move* also comes from the martial arts, in particular, the art of American Kenpo.[10] It describes a fundamental move or concept that, if learned well, can be used in a number of situations with only a little adaptation. It's the martial teaching to master a concept to learn a thousand techniques. Or, as Japanese sword master Miyamoto Musashi said, "From one thing, know ten thousand things."

It's the 80/20 rule—a few ideas that give you disproportionately great results. We have carefully chosen the 3 Master Moves on the Q2 Process Map because, if learned and applied well, they will have a significant impact on your ability to win.

We will focus our discussion of these master moves on one of the most challenging sources of the incoming that people deal with today in business—their email inbox. However, if you learn the principles behind the master moves, you can apply them in a number of ways and to a number of technologies that are conduits for the incoming, including text, social media, messaging apps, and even real people, depending on the circumstances.

MASTER MOVE 1: WIN WITHOUT FIGHTING

On the Q2 Process Map, this master move is placed between the relentless incoming and the moment of choice.

Currently, over 196 billion emails are sent and received every day. On a typical workday, individuals send and receive an average of 121 emails, and it is projected that this number will only grow.[11] It is critical that we make the right moves to turn our inbox not into the dreaded work of the day, but into an extremely useful productivity engine.

Here is the key paradigm shift around your email. Your email is not just a bunch of messages. In reality, every email is a *decision*. We said in chapter 1 that one of the most pervasive problems of the twenty-first century for knowledge workers is the sheer number of decisions that need to be made all day long. And when we are busy deleting, moving, being tempted by, or answering emails, we are using up energy that would be better applied elsewhere.

Win Without Fighting is based on the principle of automation. The goal is to confidently automate as many of these decisions as possible so that our brains do not have to use up energy on the mundane, useless, or unnecessary.

One of the most powerful ways to automate your incoming email is to master the rules or filter functions of your email program. Rules or filters can automatically put many of your emails where you want them to go before they ever hit your inbox!

For example, you can set up rules that automatically:

- Delete junk email that made it through your spam filters.
- Delete irrelevant emails that don't pertain to you.
- Prioritize the cc list and the reply all function.
- Highlight email from critical people like your boss, spouse, key team members, and so on.
- Move key reference documents, trade journals, and the like to their folders for later review.
- Move non-time-sensitive emails from certain groups of users (like people you don't know) to a custom folder for later review.
- Forward specific emails, like reports, to others.
- Auto-reply to specific senders to let them know if you are out or set expectations about when you will respond.
- Copy specific emails to different locations.

Of course, you should be aware of any corporate guidelines that govern how you handle and delete email. But by taking some Q2 time to set up these rules, you can save thousands of hours later on. Let's say, for example, that you get one hundred new emails per day. How many of them are important? Let's make the following assumptions:

- Thirty of them (30 percent) are vital and need your focused attention right away.
- Forty of them (40 percent) are important but do not require immediate action (reports, ccs, project status, etc.).
- Thirty of them (30 percent) are a waste of time and shouldn't be there at all (spam and other nonimportant items).

Let's also assume that it takes you an average of fifteen seconds just to decide what to do with each email. That means you will spend twenty-five minutes per day simply sorting your email. That's just over two hours in a five-day work week spent sorting email, not actually doing anything with it.

But let's be real. What actually happens is, as you read each email, you start to load your brain with all sorts of questions, you read and reread, and sometimes reply. Often you move on to the next email, leaving the old one to sit there for a later decision and/or action. Over time, this results in an inbox filled with hundreds of emails in various stages of uncertainty and completion, which is a source of mental stress hanging over you throughout the day.

If, however, you set up some rules that could accurately discard the 30 percent that shouldn't be there at all, automatically handle a good portion of the 40 percent that are important but not urgent, and highlight the vital 30 percent, you would have a different email experience altogether.

First, there is a bunch of stuff you wouldn't even see, because it would have been automatically deleted or filed away for you. This would allow you to reclaim much of the two hours a week you spend simply sorting.

Then, you could easily direct your attention to the messages you know are likely to be important, because your rules helped you identify them quickly.

One of our clients reported that after applying Win Without Fighting to his inbox, he went on vacation for a few days and did not check his email. When he returned, he sat at his desk, took a deep breath, opened up his email program and, with trepidation, hit the send-and-receive button. What happened next was a wonder to him. He said that he watched about three hundred emails start to pour in and, at the same time, he watched about eighty of them disappear, thanks to rules. It was a visceral example to him as he thought about how much time and effort he would have had to put in dealing with an extra eighty emails. All those decisions had been made previously and he no longer needed to spend his brain power on them. He was able to maintain his vacation glow just a little longer as he caught up on what was really important and that needed his attention.

One great best practice of managing email is to block out some Q2 time to check your email throughout the day—a Q2 Time Zone. This allows you to check every couple of hours instead of every couple of minutes. Research shows that every time you interrupt yourself and come out of the flow of your work, the recovery time required to refocus your attention gets longer and longer. With this rule, you can focus on your work and, at a natural stopping point, look up and see if anything important has come in, without having been distracted by the other thirty emails that came in while you were working.

Time zones for email may not be doable for everyone. Some people are in the position of "If my boss needs me, my boss needs me." Most technologies have features that allow you to highlight the key people whom you need to respond to. Do you need a color or a sound or a big label showing up on your screen for your boss or spouse or partner? Set up that rule so that you can put your finest attention and energy on the project at hand without constantly worrying that you will miss something from key people.

Be careful how many people you prioritize. Pick the two to three you really need to respond to immediately and no more. Otherwise, you will have a chaotic mess of dings and pings, bringing you right back to where you started—total distraction and interruption.

Think for a moment about how well you are using the rules functions of your email to Win Without Fighting. You may find that:

- You have never set up any rules at all and didn't even know that you could.
- You have set up a few rules, but haven't kept them current.
- You have set up a few rules, and realize you can automate many, many more emails.
- You have a great set of rules and actively maintain them, saving you tons of time, attention, and energy. You are an inbox ninja.

This system is not hard to set up. With just thirty minutes of Q2 time, you can set up a system of rules that will pay for itself in saved time in just a day or two. Everything after that is just an ongoing profit of reclaimed time, attention, and energy.

Once you set up your rules or filter system, continue to be intentional about keeping it current. Continue to discern your new messages through the eyes of the quadrants. Look for patterns to automate and opportunities to prioritize. When you see one, take just an additional second or two to make a rule for those messages, then they will be handled smartly from that time forward.

If your inbox is currently a total disaster, filled with several hundred (or even thousand!) emails, and you don't even know where to start, see "Inbox Detox: Help for the Seriously Buried" later in this chapter.

OPTIMIZING THIS MOVE

As we have discussed, we are focusing on your email inbox because it is a common challenge for people who work in organizations. However, the principle of Win Without Fighting can apply to lots of technologies and circumstances:

- You can use the features on your phone to set up separate ringtones for a few most important relationships and use a different ringtone for other relationships. This allows your phone to alert you differently when you get a text or phone call so that you can respond appropriately. You can also set some numbers to not to ring at all; they go right to your voicemail. You have decided from whom and how you will accept an interruption to your flow. This keeps your attention and your brain cells focused on the important task at hand.

- If you have someone to whom you can delegate tasks, this can be seen as another form of automation. Are you making all the decisions on even the smallest things, when someone on your team would be better suited to handle them so that you can free your mind for something of higher value? By spending some time and helping this person get better at handling things that might otherwise come to you, you are automatically removing those things from your inbox in the future and, as a bonus, helping others grow in their jobs as well.

- If you are lucky enough to have an assistant, this kind of thinking can help there as well. The better and more trusted that person is at his or her job, the less stuff you need to see, or at least you can see it in a sorted, organized fashion. This empowerment automatically takes care of things that would otherwise be filling your mental inbox.

THE WISE SAMURAI

Let's wrap up Master Move 1: Win Without Fighting with a famous fable from Japan.

A young samurai found himself one day on a ferry with a legendary swordsman known throughout all of Japan. Anxious to prove himself, he sought a duel with the Master. He challenged him with great confidence, shouting, "Either you or I will die!"

The Master did not respond. He had faced many challengers before and was tired of useless battles.

The young samurai was offended and shouted even louder, "Come fight me now and either you or I will die!"

Finally, after many attempts, the Master rose and said, "I accept your challenge, but there are others on this ferry who might be hurt. Let us go to that island so that we may freely fight."

The young samurai accepted the offer and stood boldly at the helm of the ferry while it moved toward the island.

As the ferry drew close, the Master graciously allowed the young samurai to step off the boat first, and then quickly steered the boat away from the island, leaving a humbled young samurai behind.

As we face the daily battles that strive to keep us from Q2, there are many battles we do not need to fight at all. If you are wise, you can Win Without Fighting and leave a lot of stuff on the island, moving on to more important things. Knowing which battles we can ignore, then setting up automatic systems to keep them from distracting us from higher purposes, is the essence of Master Move 1.

In the words of the classic military strategist Sun Tzu, "The supreme art is to subdue the enemy without fighting." [12]

MASTER MOVE 2: TURN IT INTO WHAT IT IS

Now that we have automated a percentage of the incoming, we can move to the next master move, which is positioned after the moment of choice in the Q2 Process Map. The goal of this move is to eliminate any additional Q3s and Q4s from your inbox that rules and filters did not handle, then effectively manage the Q1s and Q2s.

For many people, this work can still represent a large and overwhelming number of emails. Getting this fixed is important not only for your productivity, but to your health as well. A recent study found that email can increase the physical components of stress including elevated blood pressure, heart rate, and levels of the hormone cortisol. Interestingly, the study also found that:

Emails which were irrelevant, which interrupted work or demanded an immediate response were particularly taxing, while those which arrived in response to completed work had a calming effect. Filing emails into folders also lowered levels of stress and prompted a sense of well-being because it helped people feel in control.[13]

Take a moment and assess how you are managing your email inbox today. Do some of these behaviors sound familiar?

- I read an email and say to myself, "I'll get to it later," only to have it scrolled away and out of sight.
- I read an email, then mark it unread so I can make sure that I deal with it later.
- I move emails to subfolders to keep my inbox clear, only to end up worrying if I actually did what I was supposed to do (e.g., boss-folder emails).
- I print out emails that are to-dos and keep a pile on my desk to get to sometime.
- I use my inbox as a filing system and keep everything there. I use the search function if I need to look up old emails. I just hope that I haven't missed anything important in the process.
- I panic when my boss calls and says, "Did you get my email?" I frantically scroll to find it in the email gravel.
- I have a pervasive sense of unease because my inbox is chaos.
- I am essentially living out of my inbox.

So how many emails do you have in your inbox right now, both read and unread? Hundreds? Thousands? Some companies have started to automatically empty out employee inboxes every thirty or sixty days because the volume on the servers is so large. That might sound terrible, but it forces people to clean out their inboxes and save their stuff by archiving before the big deletion. Although archiving is good, archiving hundreds and thousands of emails is still overwhelming and does not help you get the right things accomplished.

To understand Master Move 2, realize that every email is really only made up of one or more of the Core 4: an appointment, a task, a contact, or a note/document. When you look at each email with this new pair of glasses, you realize that the information in the email already has a place set up in your Core 4 system where such information should go.

A typical email, for instance, may look something like this:

To: Jaime
Cc: Tomaso
From: Kiyomi
Subject: For the Meeting Next Week

Jaime,

First, nice to meet you. I look forward to getting together next week and getting up to speed. Can you please review the attached with your team and make sure the results for Brazil and Argentina are right? I need this back by the end of next week.

Thanks,
Kiyomi

<<attachment>>

Many people, when they get an email like this, will scan it quickly and leave it in their inbox with all the other emails so that they can get back to it later.

Take a minute right now and see if you can break the above email down into the Core 4 for Jaime. Which category or categories of information does that email represent?

- **Appointment:** Jaime needs to schedule a meeting with his team to review the results for Brazil and Argentina.
- **Task:** Jaime needs to review the numbers before he meets with his team.
- **Contact:** Kiyomi is new, and Jaime needs to store contact information.
- **Note/Document:** Jaime needs to keep the attached document to review later.

Once you've identified each of the Core 4, then *immediately* Turn It Into What It Is and get it *out* of your inbox. The basic rule here is to touch it once. Here's how you can do it.

First, add the appointment to your calendar. If you are using a program like Outlook, Google, or IBM Notes, there is great functionality to allow this to happen very easily. In many cases, with a click of a button, you can create a meeting and get it onto your and others' calendars. You will find, in most cases, that the conversation threads and even attachments will go along for the ride into the appointment. This makes it even easier to get it out of the inbox.

Next, Jaime needs to review the numbers before he meets with his team. That is a *task,* and with some dragging, dropping, or the click of a menu item in your system, that email can be turned into a task and put on your Master Task List. In most cases, you can put a start and/or due date on the task and assign a priority rating.

When creating a task, we strongly recommend you start the title of the task with an action verb. Our task lists are long and, by the time we get to the task, if it just says "Brazil numbers," we may not remember what we were supposed to do with the numbers. Using the action verb makes it specific: "Review Brazil/Argentina numbers."

Next, Jaime does not yet have Kiyomo's contact information. Many times we see people cutting and pasting in a new contact when, in fact, your system may have easy menu items to immediately turn the sender into a contact, populating a few of the contact fields without your having to do another thing. Whatever the approach, get this information into your system for contacts.

Finally, you also need to store the document in your electronic system for notes/documents so that you can have it when you need it. (We'll show you some even more powerful ways to do this when we get to Master Move 3: Link to Locate.)

Now that we have turned this email into what it is, using the Core 4, we can confidently delete the email!

Because you have been intentional about turning things into what they are, nothing is lost. Everything is in its right place and easily accessible to act on when the time is right. This will help you clear the clutter from your inbox and give you greater peace of mind. It will keep you working in the important but not urgent Q2 mode. Also, when Q1 crises do come up, you will be better prepared to handle them because everything will be in order and you won't be caught off guard.

Having an uncluttered inbox gives you an uncluttered mind. There is nothing more peaceful than seeing your number of messages reduced to just a few and knowing that everything is where it belongs.

But be careful not to go too far in the other direction. Don't land in Q3 and Q4 because you are turning *everything* into the Core 4. Don't turn an email into something just because, when you actually could just get rid of it. Use the five-second rule, meaning that if you can handle the situation or respond quickly to a question right now, do it, particularly if you have blocked time to clear out your inbox. Stay conscious during the process so that you don't get lost in any particular item. If it starts to take longer, turn it into your Core 4 for attention later.

Because this master move helps us put important information in an organized system, when we do our Weekly and Daily Q2 Planning, we can easily see what needs to be done. We have a robust and complete Master Task List, we have key appointments on our calendar, and we know where our important contacts, notes, and documents are. As a result, we are able to make thoughtful and accurate choices and focus our attention on our Big Rocks.

The first two master moves work together and have been game-changing for many of our clients. One person said,

> I was so pumped about all the new things I learned about my inbox and calendar, I spent Friday evening organizing. Just now, I'm down from 19,000-plus emails in my inbox to zero! I have rules, files, and subfiles made. Being organized makes me so happy, and I had no idea how much my inbox was stressing me out every morning.

Another said,

Doing the initial purge of my 7,500 emails was one thing, but I wanted to let you know that two weeks after your webinar, I have only one email in my inbox—and I consider that one too many! I have never been this in control for this long. I can't imagine ever going back.

Once you understand the power of these first two master moves, you will make your inbox work for you instead of the other way around. Again, if you have a system like Outlook, Google, or IBM Notes, there is already some integration between your email, calendars, and task lists, which can make this second master move even easier.

OPTIMIZING THIS MOVE

When you become adept at Master Move 2: Turn It Into What It Is, you might actually want to *encourage* people to send emails so you can put them through the Turn It Into What It Is process. For instance,

- If someone approaches you and asks if you and your finance partner can join tomorrow morning's meeting at ten, you might ask him to send you either an email with the specifics or a meeting invitation, so you can easily get these things onto your calendar.
- If someone you are having lunch with asks if you have time to review some research for her, and you choose to do it, ask her to send you an email with the documents attached, so that you can turn it into a task.

When you are practiced at this master move, you begin to see every bit of incoming as one of the Core 4. With or without technology, your natural response to everything is to Turn It Into What It Is. For example:

- You get a text to pick up some milk and fresh bread on the way home, so you immediately get it onto your task list. If it is electronic, you might even put a reminder on it to make extra sure that you will have a good evening!
- You see a billboard with details for a new musical that will be coming to town—one you've always wanted to see. You don't just let this information sit in your head. You get it onto your Master Task List! (If you are driving, pull over to do it safely!)
- You found some recipes you think you might want to tackle someday. So you put them in your notes, instead of letting them disappear into ominous piles of paper in your kitchen cabinet.

The whole point of this is, since you have a robust system to handle the Core 4, when you come across information that is important, take just a moment to put it into that system so that it becomes part of your Q2 Planning process and is available when you need it.

MASTER MOVE 3: LINK TO LOCATE

Have you ever been late for a meeting because you were scrambling to find all the resources you needed? Or have you ever done a great job blocking out two hours to work on a project, but spent the first half hour looking for all the right information?

When you are busy looking for stuff, which quadrant are you in? Generally, it's a self-imposed Q1. We have higher-value uses for our time, and that is what Master Move 3: Link to Locate helps you solve.

The paradigm shift for this move is to see the relatedness of information and to proactively connect resources among the Core 4 as much as you can ahead of time so you don't have to search for them later. It's based on the principle of preparation and, in most cases, it doesn't take long at all.

Even though many search functions have become quite effective for digital information, the more key information you have organized and linked, the lower your risk of not finding what you need, the greater your confidence, and the sooner your attention can be focused on the important work at hand. Plus, search functions don't work with information on paper!

Linking can be done by:

- Inserting the actual file.
- Inserting an active hyperlink.
- Creating a text-based link.

Here are some examples of how this works:

- John has a meeting coming up in a few weeks, and he knows he will need some reports for that meeting. So instead of waiting until the last minute, he drops those electronic documents into the appointment on his calendar so that, when he gets to the meeting, he just needs to click to bring up that information.
- If John is concerned about creating a duplicate of a document, which he would do by dropping it into his appointment, some

programs will let him create an active hyperlink to that document, which is stored elsewhere on his hard drive. That way, when he clicks on it, it opens the original file. He could also copy and paste a hyperlink to an article he read on the Web that has some information relevant to his meeting. That way, when he arrives at the meeting, he just clicks the link in his appointment and the information is there.

- Suppose John has a paper-based system or needs to bring some other files that are not on his hard drive or network. In this case, he could use a text-based link (similar to a hyperlink) to remind him of what he needs to bring and where it is. In other words, he could type a reference like this in the body of his appointment:

    <Marketing File/Quarterly Reports/Market Pricing Report>

    The angle brackets at the start and the end of this reference let him know there is information linked to this meeting. This note tells him what and where the information is (Marketing File/Quarterly Reports) and which ultimate document he is looking for (Market Pricing Report). The format of this is similar to a hyperlink tab used on the Web or that you might see in the URL at the top of your browser. The only difference is that John is typing it in, since it refers to something he can't actually click on to retrieve.

You can use any format. The principle is simply to get your stuff together ahead of time while you are thinking about it so that you don't have to search for it later, when it may not be as fresh in your mind.

There are lots of variations of this technique. For example:

- If you are setting up a group meeting and there is a document everyone needs to review, be sure to attach it to the meeting. That way, everyone will easily have access to it and won't have to ask you for it later.
- If you are invited to a group meeting and have some personal documents you want to bring but that *don't* pertain to others, you can create a second, parallel appointment at the same time that only shows up on your calendar. Label it "Documents for the Meeting," and link to them there. That way, they are right there at the meeting, but available only to you.
- You may have a financial report on a server that is shared and constantly updated by others, but which you need to reference every week in your team meeting. Most programs will allow you to create a link to that document and put it in your repeating appointment so that, every week, you can just click the link and see the most current data.

The number of links you add is entirely up to you. The point is to not get obsessed with links, turning this into a Q4 activity, but to proactively create some well-chosen cross-references that will help you connect different items ahead of time.

OPTIMIZING THIS MOVE WITH TAGS

A number of applications are now using various forms of tags as a way to organize and connect information. You can use this tagging function to create links as well.

Say, for instance, that you have a note-taking/document-management app on your devices that uses tags. You can easily create a set of tags that relate to these marketing meetings. That way, any note that you want to have at your fingertips for the marketing meeting could be tagged "Marketing Meeting." That way, no matter what other categories these documents may be in, all you need to do is type the name of that tag in your program, and all those documents will show up. Depending on your application or your own preferences, you could also use the hashtag symbol to remind you that it is a tag in your system; for example, <#MarketingMeeting> or just #MarketingMeeting.

This is taking us back to the idea of swordlessness. The master can continue to win the battle as technologies change, because her strength is in her knowledge of the underlying paradigms and principles. The specific tools and technologies are secondary.

INBOX DETOX: HELP FOR THE SERIOUSLY BURIED

So where do you start? You might be thinking, "I have thousands of emails, and it will take me forever to make a dent." If you are feeling overwhelmed by your inbox and need to take some drastic action, here is a three-step plan to come clean and get back in charge. It takes about two hours, is actually easier than you think it is, and is definitely worth the effort.

Step 1: Create a subfolder in your inbox called Detox.

Step 2: Take everything from your inbox, except the most recent two hundred messages, and move it to your Detox folder. Now, you only have two hundred messages in your inbox.

Step 3: Review the remaining two hundred items and either

- Delete them.
- Create a specific rule to handle them in the future.
- Turn them into appointments, tasks, contacts, or notes so you can work on them later—then delete them!

Or

- Respond to them immediately, if you can do it in a minute or less.

Handling these two hundred messages shouldn't take too long, because you are simply organizing where they go. You are not taking any time now to act on them, unless it can be done in a minute or less. By following these three steps, you have cleaned out your inbox and set up some basic rules to keep your inbox clean.

If, for some reason, you need to access an email from your Detox folder, you can search for it there. (That's what you've been doing already!) Chances are, you won't need to do that too often, and now your inbox is clean and you have a fresh start!

To stay on top of this, you should schedule a regular time to handle your email and diligently set up new rules for messages as you encounter them. Pretty soon you'll have a well-functioning, ninja-worthy inbox working for you.

THE Q2 EMAIL MANIFESTO:
ESTABLISHING EMAIL PROTOCOLS

One of the best things you can do to win the broader email battle in your organization is to create common protocols around email and other forms of communication. This is especially vital if you are the boss, but if you are not, you can still work within your circle of influence to change the nature of the incoming inside your team or organization.

For example, does your company suffer from reply-all disease? For some reason, it seems like this is a mindless response all over the world. What about ccs? Do you find yourself on every distribution list in the company? What about the thank-you emails? How many iterations of thank you and you're welcome do you have? Here's a sample Q2 manifesto you can use or modify to identify a set of communication protocols to be used inside your organization.

OUR Q2 EMAIL MANIFESTO

We agree to help each other stay in Q2 and
consciously avoid Q3s, Q4s, and unnecessary Q1s
by adhering to the following protocols. We will

- Consciously decide if an email really needs to be sent. Is it putting others into Q3, Q4, or Q1?
- Use Q1 or Q2 in the subject line when possible to help people determine their priorities.
- Hit reply all only when absolutely necessary.
- Review our distribution lists to ensure they are up to date with the right names.
- Only include cc if it is truly necessary for that person to receive a copy.
- Make sure the purpose of the email is clear in the subject line.
- Keep emails as short as possible to get the best response.
- Pick up the phone to discuss the issue after two or a maximum of three rounds of a conversation thread.
- Be judicious about what is critical, and only mark emails with "high importance" or "high priority" when they really are.
- Establish expected response times. We will not send people an email, then interrupt them fifteen minutes later to see if they got it. That's a Q3.

While this manifesto focuses on email, there are lots of other forms of communication (like text or chat) that need to have boundaries and ground rules. You can add these to your manifesto, as they apply to you and your organization.

You can also apply this idea to family members and others. Take time to clarify what they can expect when they try to reach you during work hours or at other times. Working together to define these expectations can save a lot of frustration and prevent relationship damage.

One area where clear expectations can help is around off-hours communication. Say, for example, that you receive an email or a text from your boss late at night, asking you to do something, get something, or research something. Does he or she expect you to do it now? Are you going to sleep worried? The digital fact of constant accessibility has created wildly different realities for people in managing how their work and personal lives fit together in a balanced way.

One executive we know, who catches up on emails at night, has been clear with her team that they are to ignore any after-hours emails from her unless there is a Q1 in the subject line. And, in that case, it has to be something really important. There is not much that cannot wait until the morning or the beginning of the week. In addition, she never texts after hours. After-hours texting creates a sense of urgency that makes it hard to resist peeking, so why create stress in other people's lives? Establishing clear expectations as to how to deal with these communications can save you and others a lot of stress.

For more information on how setting up common protocols can help you establish a Q2 culture in your organization, be sure to read the chapter "Building a Q2 Culture in Your Organization."

Q2 PRODUCTIVITY ACCELERATORS: THERE'S AN APP FOR EVERYTHING!

No chapter on technology would be complete without addressing the world of apps and mobile devices.

The *great* news is that there are many inexpensive or free high-quality apps for almost anything you can think of.

The *bad* news is that there are many inexpensive or free high-quality apps for almost anything you can think of.

What a multitude of essentially free, interesting, and instantly available apps does is lower the threshold for interruption and distraction from these technologies. There is very little ROI calculation that goes into the decision to try an app unless we bring it ourselves. That's why app stores are so successful!

However, now that you have a clear understanding of Q2 and the cost of distraction, as well as an awareness of your natural tendency to look at new, shiny objects, you can bring discernment to this source of incoming as well.

With a clear view of your Q2 Roles and Goals, take a discerning look at your current portfolio of applications on your smartphone and tablet. Are they Q2, or Q3 and Q4? What should you remove and what should you keep? What should you be adding, now that you know the ground rules of effective technology and productivity?

When you look at your apps through the lens of the Time Matrix, you can see that there are a number of apps that are very productive. They save you time and money, and help you achieve important goals. Travel apps, fitness apps, news apps, personal-finance apps, social-media apps, and so forth can help you accelerate your efforts in these areas. There are even some great games that can help you relax.

The point here is to apply the same principles to apps that you do to other forms of technology. This will allow you to create a conscious collection of resources that help you move forward, rather than a private set of distractions that keep you from paying attention to the things that really matter.

WINNING THE BATTLE

Mastering the skills of any martial art takes time, effort, practice, mistakes, and even more practice, but the return on investment is exponential. The Q2 Process Map is designed to help you eliminate the unnecessary incoming and protect the Big Rocks in the midst of all the gravel. It helps to provide you with the necessary perspective, so when things get tough and crazy, you are able to make good decisions about how you will invest your attention and energy.

In the end, the most important asset in any conflict is a calm and undisturbed state of mind. This allows you to act fluidly and with discernment in the moment of choice. While the skills we have taught in this chapter are important, even more vital is your own ability to transcend your natural impulse to respond to every beep and buzz, and to consciously act from a centered, clear-thinking Q2 perspective.

As famed Japanese historical writer Eiji Yoshikawa said, "A serious student is more concerned with training his mind and disciplining his spirit than with developing martial skills."

By regularly practicing the elements of the Q2 Process Map, you can strengthen your Q2 mindset and focus like a master on the larger, more important things in your life.

SIMPLE WAYS TO GET STARTED

You can begin applying the principles and practices of Choice 4: Rule Your Technology, Don't Let It Rule You by taking any of the following simple actions. Pick the ones that work best for you.

- Look at where you are keeping your Core 4. Pick one of them and find a better way to manage that information.
- Take fifteen minutes and set up some rules to handle your most distracting or critical emails.
- Take five emails and turn them into what they are.
- Look ahead and find one upcoming meeting where you will need some documents. Link those documents to that meeting.
- Take two hours and do an inbox detox.
- Go to Appendix A: Top 25 Email Protocols and look at some protocol ideas there. Pick two or three, and see if other members of your team will join you in implementing them.

TO SUM UP

- Technology can accelerate the inflow of gravel into our lives, burying us faster under a mountain of less important things.
- Strive for the martial ideal of swordlessness. Master the underlying principles and skills that will enable you to use any technology in a Q2 way.
- See order in the chaos, and sort incoming information into four categories: appointments, tasks, contacts, and notes/documents.
- When you use a paper system: Everything in one place. When you use an electronic system: Everything in every place.
- Defend with the 3 Master Moves: Win Without Fighting, Turn It Into What It Is, and Link to Locate.
- Create a Q2 manifesto with your family or your team.
- Use the principles of the 5 Choices to choose your apps.

ENERGY MANAGEMENT

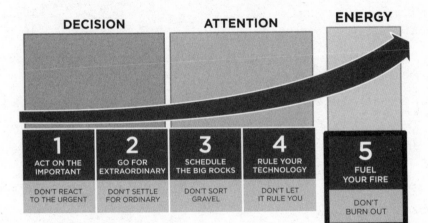

DECISION

ATTENTION

ENERGY

1
ACT ON THE IMPORTANT

DON'T REACT TO THE URGENT

2
GO FOR EXTRAORDINARY

DON'T SETTLE FOR ORDINARY

3
SCHEDULE THE BIG ROCKS

DON'T SORT GRAVEL

4
RULE YOUR TECHNOLOGY

DON'T LET IT RULE YOU

5
FUEL YOUR FIRE

DON'T BURN OUT

FUEL YOUR FIRE,
DON'T BURN OUT

The energy of the mind is the essence of life.

—Aristotle

Marianne, a good friend of ours, found herself at a crossroad in her career. She was a hard-working, high-level executive but was in constant pain and her brain felt foggy all day. Because of her decreased ability to think clearly, she had begun to lose confidence in her ability to make important decisions, and even had begun to forget important information. At first, she assumed that she was just getting older, and that this happened to everyone. As the symptoms got worse, so did her anxiety about her job and her ability to continue to perform in her leadership role. She worried about the people who depended on her decisions and began to fear that she would eventually be fired for not being able to do what her job required. Rather than go through that, she thought that she would simply quit.

One day, while she was dealing with this deep worry about her future, her daughter recommended some brain-healthy foods and exercise patterns she was studying with a doctor. Thinking that there was nothing to lose, Marianne went to see the doctor and began to change her habits of diet, sleep, and exercise to more brain-healthy patterns. Over the course of two months, she began to feel a noticeable decrease in pain and a dramatic difference in her energy and clarity of mind. Within a year, she had lost fifty pounds and felt younger, sharper, and more energized than she had for decades. More important, she has continued in her leadership role in her company and has become an even more dynamic and compelling leader than she was before.

Throughout this book, we have targeted the brain as the number-one asset and tool that must be optimized. To be extraordinarily productive, we need to create a way of life that is intentional, consciously making the highest-value decisions virtually every waking minute of the day. We need to cultivate the state of mind that allows us to detect the subtle thoughts about what matters in our work and lives, and make choices to schedule and execute those things first. We need to be sensitive to the answers to questions like "Is this important?" "Is it aligned to my most important roles and goals?" "Do I have the most important things scheduled in my week and day so that I can get them done in the midst of the gravel?" "Am I controlling all the temptations my gadgetry brings me in order to avoid unnecessary Q3s and Q4s?"

All of this conscious effort takes extraordinary brainpower. Using your Thinking Brain to be conscious throughout the day takes a load of energy. Although your brain is only about 2 percent of your body weight, it takes about 20 percent of your total energy.[1] In addition, stressful tasks affect moods, feelings, and other brain-related functions that can tax your ability to think clearly and make wise decisions.

If we are going to master the skills of Choices 1 to 4, then fueling our brain with the large amounts of oxygen and steady glucose it requires is the most important Q2 activity on the list. Unfortunately, in today's world, it is last on the list in many cases.

ARE YOU HAVING AN ENERGY CRISIS?

Our mode of life today—constant stress, poor diet, lack of exercise and sleep—leads to what scientists call *exhaustion syndrome*. The rest of us call it *burnout*. We continually push through each day, postponing the renewal time our brains and bodies need. The mantra is "Work like crazy, then crash." It even becomes a badge of honor to brag, "Our team was up until midnight." "I worked through the whole weekend." "Vacation? Are you crazy? No time!" In the end, this pattern is killing our brain's capacity to make good decisions and our brain's capacity in general. In addition, if we work in Quadrants 1 and 3 all day, strung out on urgencies and emergencies, we naturally end up in Quadrant 4, defaulting to mindlessly excessive activity. This is the brain's way of saying it has been way overtaxed and needs time to rejuvenate. All it can stand are the most basic tasks that are nonthreatening and mindless; this might feel rewarding in the moment, but in the long term, it is just waste.

By contrast, extraordinarily productive people consistently recharge. They have a more constant feeling of energy and capability throughout the day. Because they have a Quadrant 2 mentality around this, they maintain a regular flow of fuel to the mind and body so they can perform at their best, and they have established habits that add fuel to their fire so that they don't burn out.

The purpose of this chapter is to help you have the energy to maintain a thoughtful, conscious approach to the choices you make and carry out so that you can feel accomplished at the end of every day.

THE POWER OF PURPOSE

Your mental energy comes from two basic sources: a powerful purpose and your physical body.

Remember the work on your Q2 Role Statement in Choice 2? Half the work in thinking about what a vision of success looks like in your most important roles is to find your purpose—your motivation in the great contributions you can make. This generates tremendous amounts of energy and power as you work to feel accomplished in these roles every day.

Motivation comes from the Latin word *movere*, which means to move. It takes energy to move things, and a motivating vision can call forth incredible effort, even when we otherwise wouldn't make it.

You may have heard stories where people push above and beyond what they think they can do because of the power of a deeper motivation or goal. These deeper sources can become more available in your life, constantly pulsing through your daily activities. This happens when what you are doing is consciously aligned with your highest purposes and aspirations in your Q2 Roles.

According to Daniel Pink, there are numerous studies showing that people who operate from a sense of internal motivation experience "higher self-esteem, better interpersonal relationships, and greater general well-being"[2] than those who do not have these intrinsic sources of motivation. He summarizes the research further by stating, "The most deeply motivated people—not to mention those who are most productive and satisfied—hitch their desires to a cause larger than themselves."[3]

While working without a compelling purpose can be a drain to our brain's energy, working with a strong sense of purpose can connect the deeper, emotional parts of our brain to our own specific intentions and higher causes so that our brain becomes more in sync. This is vital for our personal lives as well, which can often take a back seat to our busy work lives. Q2 Roles and Q2 Role Statements allow us to rethink our personal roles and find untapped energy to get them accomplished. When this happens, we experience greater mental congruity and clarity, while at the same time increasing the level of meaning and fulfillment in all we do.

FIVE DRIVERS OF MENTAL AND PHYSICAL ENERGY

While a powerful purpose matters immensely, over the long run, a powerful purpose alone won't cut it. Without a second, physical source of energy, you are still at risk of hitting a wall.

You see this in people who are excited about their goals but don't have the physical or mental energy to carry them through. Or people who power through a project, while saying to themselves, "I know I will need a week to recover from this." Or people who regularly spend all their energy during the week, then simply crash on the weekend because they have nothing left.

In the end, when our bodies and brains are running on empty, it affects our desire and purpose as well. When we feel we can't achieve our goals, we end up lowering our sights and, in extreme cases, give in to depression and despair.

To maintain your ability to carry out your great purposes and make the day-to-day decisions that get you there, you need the sustainable physical energy that comes from a well-cared-for and well-functioning body to fuel the brain with lots of oxygen and a consistent flow of glucose.

The steps to a healthy brain are not rocket science. Our parents and experts have been telling us what we need to do for years, but when you look through the lens of your need for consistent high-value decision making and attention focus in the twenty-first century, the drivers of good brain health take on a whole new importance.

The 5 Energy Drivers are illustrated in the diagram below:

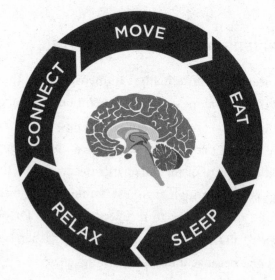

1. **Move.** It's not just about exercise. Your body was meant to move, and it turns out that all sorts of good things happen to your brain when you move around a lot, and a lot of bad things happen to your brain when you don't.

2. **Eat.** Just as you don't put dirt in your car's gas tank, you shouldn't put poor-quality food in your body. The food you eat is like fuel for your brain. There are some simple eating guidelines you can follow that will help you fuel your brain for optimal performance.

3. **Sleep.** Sleep is where you consolidate learning, improve memory, and subconsciously sort out complex data and decisions. Getting a good night's sleep is not just enjoyable, it is vital to extraordinary productivity.

4. **Relax.** Our "stressed out" environment can be a huge brain drain. Learning to turn off the stress responses in our brain and act from a more centered, relaxed state can have a tremendous impact on our performance.

5. **Connect.** The brain fundamentally requires positive social connections for survival, and such connections are a huge source of energy. Spending time building and maintaining meaningful relationships is actually nourishing to our brain.

We will explore each of these sources of energy and provide practical tips on how to tap into these clean, renewable energy sources in your life. First, take this brief self-assessment to determine how you are doing on these five drivers. Circle the number that represents where you are on the scale.

QUESTIONS	Not Like Me at All								A Lot Like Me	
1. I get up and move regularly throughout the work day.	1	2	3	4	5	6	7	8	9	10
2. I have a consistent exercise program that boosts my energy.	1	2	3	4	5	6	7	8	9	10
3. I eat in ways that provide sustained energy throughout the day.	1	2	3	4	5	6	7	8	9	10
4. I have a pattern of eating nutritious food at every meal.	1	2	3	4	5	6	7	8	9	10
5. I get at least seven hours of sleep each night.	1	2	3	4	5	6	7	8	9	10
6. I am satisfied with the quality of sleep I get each night.	1	2	3	4	5	6	7	8	9	10
7. I have effective coping strategies to deal with stress.	1	2	3	4	5	6	7	8	9	10
8. My lifestyle supports my ability to manage stress.	1	2	3	4	5	6	7	8	9	10
9. I take time to connect regularly with the important people in my life.	1	2	3	4	5	6	7	8	9	10
10. I regularly connect with the purposes and values that make my life meaningful.	1	2	3	4	5	6	7	8	9	10
TOTAL SCORE										

As a general rule, if your score is below 65, there are probably a number of things you might do to boost your mental energy. If you are low in one or more of these areas, you may want to pay particular attention to that driver in this chapter. If you are low on a lot of them, don't worry. Learn more about each one, then pick the one on which you want to start. Once you feel accomplished with one, you will be motivated to tackle another.

DRIVER 1: MOVE

We've often heard that exercise is good for us, and that is certainly true. There is plenty of research supporting the idea that regular exercise will improve memory, brain health, and physical fitness.

Many people know they need to do a better job at this. If this is you, then it probably requires a Q2 Goal and a Q2 Time Zone to make it an important recurring Q2 activity for you every week.

Research also shows that exercise is not enough for the brain's health.

Even if you are a regular exerciser, you can completely reverse the benefits of your exercise by sitting in your chair all day long. Given that many of us have jobs where we sit at a desk all day and work with a computer, this is a sobering fact.

SITTING IS THE NEW SMOKING

The research can be summarized by the popular phrase, "Sitting is the new smoking." While we may or may not agree with the comparison, we should take the concept seriously. Our brains are in a symbiotic relationship with our bodies to fuel mental and physical energy. Your brain and the rest of your body work together in elaborate and amazing ways to help you get from one place to another. It is an integrated movement system.

When your body is not moving, your brain goes on standby, because a lot of what it was designed to do is not happening. This lack of motion releases chemicals that put your body to sleep. They decrease blood flow to your brain, lower your alertness, and impair your thinking and judgment.

Dr. Ratey of Harvard Medical School says, "We're getting a new study every other week showing that even if you are in shape and you exercise, sitting kills your brain cells."[4] He goes on to say:

When you stand, your brain is acting 7 percent more effectively than when you sit because the large skeletal muscles are activated. Standing turns on the frontal cortex so you can think more clearly . . . the biggest challenge is to establish a routine and a ritual. We know how hard this is, but once you start, it takes on a life of its own.[5]

We are built to move. Our distant ancestors walked every-where, and we are physiologically programmed to walk six to seven kilometers a day. It's a biological fact: An active body is essential for sustaining energy to the brain.[6]

Look at some of the ideas that follow and assess your move-ment through the day. Are you doing any of these consciously or subconsciously? Great! If you are not, or even if you are, pick one or two more and see if you can integrate them into your daily routine.

- Take brain breaks periodically throughout the day. Get up from your chair at least every ninety minutes to walk around, even if it's just to the beverage area.
- Take the stairs, not the elevator.
- Take a walk on your lunch hour.
- Park a little farther from the entrance to work or the mall.
- Have a walking meeting.

A friend recently told us:

Sometimes if I'm at my desk and my judgment is unclear, all I need to do is stand up, walk around for a bit to shake things off, return to the issue a few minutes later, and the answer becomes obvious. I've become a great fan of doing things that keep me moving throughout the day because of how it helps me think!

What are other creative ways to integrate movement into your day, given your work environment?

> Dr. Ted Eytan of Washington, D.C., holds meetings on foot. He calls it "WWW—Working While Walking." When you're sched- uled to meet with someone, ask permission to try doing it on foot. If the answer is "Sure!" meet the person at the appointed time and just start walking. You can have a destination in mind, like the nearest coffee place, or not. You'll not only get business done, you' ll enjoy a different kind of relationship building. There is something about sharing a walk with someone.[7]

SO, WHAT ABOUT EXERCISE?

Movement throughout the day combined with a good exercise regimen is, without question, the ideal. Both are essential to op- timizing brain and body energy. Exercise, particularly aerobic exercise, can actually change the physical structure of your brain. It increases your ability to move blood, oxygen, and glucose to this energy-hungry organ. The more active you are, the more dopamine receptors in your brain, giving you better powers of concentration. Dr. Ratey states, "Nothing helps the growth of new brain cells more than aerobic exercise."[8]

A lot of what works for you depends on your age and current level of fitness. Of course, you should always involve your doctor in making decisions about changing your level of exercise, but if you are interested in vigorous physical activity, don't shy away. The latest exercise research indicates that intensity as well as variety has the biggest impact on your overall level of fitness, even for older people.[9]

Whether it's running, participation in an organized sport, a workout at the gym, swimming, free weights, or even a hardcore workout at the local CrossFit Box, there are plenty of ways to raise your body's level of fitness. Whatever your age, you can do something.

> Seventy-two-year-old brain scientist Richard Restak walks at least three times per week "for half an hour to forty-five minutes at a brisk pace in different locations around the city. That way I combine exercise with new surroundings, which keeps mental activity high. . . ." [10]

> "It's never too late," says Dr. Ratey. "I know of ninety-three-year-olds whose brains change when they start exercising. If you're in middle age and you start an exercise program, you'll push back your brain age ten to fifteen years." [11]

Even if you are young and feel healthy, a sedentary lifestyle will affect you, laying a foundation of weakness for your future.

> Ajay was an intense, hard-working young executive in his thirties. He loved his work, and devoted a lot of time and energy to it. He was used to this kind of pace and had kept it during his undergraduate and business-school years and throughout his career. Increasingly, though, he found himself tired in the evenings and almost without energy on the weekends. This was starting to affect his young family, and even his work. He had frequent headaches and muscle aches, but his only response had been to dial up the intensity and continue to push through.
> That all changed when he went to an extended family gathering one summer where one of his family members had invited

a friend who was a personal trainer. The trainer started talking about the research on the impacts of a sedentary lifestyle and, especially, what happens to your body when you spend excessive time sitting. Ajay realized that he fit the description perfectly. In fact, he had spent much of the time at the gathering sitting on the couch because he was too tired and worn out from the previous week to do anything else. What went through his mind was this: "I am only in my thirties, for crying out loud, and I feel like an invalid old man! I am sick of it!"

The next week, he went to the personal trainer, who conducted a thorough physical assessment. The trainer had Ajay perform some simple exercises, and the result confirmed Ajay's own experience—he was a mess. The trainer even found muscles in Ajay's shoulders and back that were no longer firing because his poor sitting posture had rendered them essentially useless. Ajay was determined to fix this. The impact on his life was just too great.

Over the next several months, and at considerable cost, Ajay worked closely with the trainer. They started with simple stabilizing exercises and focused on getting some of his key muscles working again. At the start, the exercises were so low weight that they were almost embarrassing, but he realized that he didn't have the muscle strength to do anything else. He needed to rebuild the foundation of health he had lost. Over a couple of months, and with the trainer's coaching, his strength and energy began to return. Ajay then began to get involved in some sports he used to enjoy when he was younger. He reorganized his schedule so that these things became a priority.

Now, in his forties, Ajay says he has never been more fit. His continued discipline in making these Q2 investments in his health and energy each week has made all the difference. He enjoys his work again and has greater energy for the other areas of his life as well. His commitment to rebuilding his physical strength became the foundation for a whole new life experience.

Ajay's experience is not unique. We know many people who have hit the Q1 wall with their health and had a wake-up moment when they realized that they needed to change. The good news is that if you regularly spend time in Q2 working on this driver, you can enjoy the benefits of physical and mental health and will not need to experience the pain of hitting the wall.

When it comes to exercise and movement, remember the symbiotic energy relationship between your brain and body! What helps your body helps your brain.

DRIVER 2: EAT

Another great way to fuel your brain is through what you eat. As Dr. Daniel Amen, one of our collaborators and a leading thinker on food and the brain, says:

> You can use food to have better mental energy during the day, but you have to be smart about it. A lot of people, when they get stressed, self-medicate with things that are bad for them, like high-sugar foods or alcohol. The most effective way to deal with stress is to eat a healthy diet, because it will balance your blood sugar.

What Dr. Amen is describing is rooted in the chemistry of the brain.

The brain runs on glucose. So, when feeling tired or worn out, what many people do is go for that quick hit of sugar (or caffeine or other stimulant) to make their brain feel good again. But what happens is that this provides a surge to the brain that generally drops us lower than when we started, creating what is known as a crash. And this pattern damages our body and brain. It may get us through the day in the short term, but it's a poor substitute for the sustained healthy energy we need for clear thinking and high performance.

What our brain really needs is a steady supply of glucose that comes from high-quality food sources. Again, in today's world, it's a Q2 choice to make this happen, but the payoff is exponential in terms of our productivity and how we feel throughout the day.

Here are some guidelines that can help you eat in a more brain-friendly way:

1. **Eat high-quality calories.** Calories are important, but maintaining good health is not as simple as balancing the number of calories in versus the number of calories out. As an overall rule, focus on eating high-quality calories. Dr. Amen says, "One cinnamon roll can cost you 720 calories and will drain your brain, whereas a 400-calorie salad made of spinach, salmon, blueberries, apples, walnuts, and red bell peppers will supercharge your energy and make you smarter."[12]

    If our diet is made up primarily of highly processed, low-nutrient foods, it is entirely possible to be overfed and undernourished. Additionally, such a diet can actually increase physical and mental stress as your body works to derive nutrition from low-quality calories and process all the artificial stuff that can show up in our food supply.[13]

Remember this simple guideline: High-quality calories tend to come from farms, not factories, and should be consumed as close to their natural state as possible.

2. **Drink plenty of water.** Your brain is 80 percent water. Anything that dehydrates it, such as too much caffeine or too much alcohol, decreases your thinking and impairs your judgment. As neuroscientist Joshua Gowin states:

> Our brains depend on proper hydration to function optimally. Brain cells require a delicate balance between water and various elements to operate, and when you lose too much water, that balance is disrupted. Your brain cells lose efficiency.[14]

To stay adequately hydrated, drink plenty of water. A good rule of thumb is to drink eight to ten glasses or about two liters of water every day.

3. **Use healthy fats.** Once you account for the water, 60 percent of the solid material in the brain is fat. Fats are actually essential for our brain, but you should focus on the healthy fats. These are the unsaturated fats found in avocados, olive oil, canola oil, peanut oil, safflower oil, corn oil, nuts (such as almonds, cashews, and pistachios), and some fish.

While consuming too much fat can be unhealthy, diets that are too low in fat can also be unhealthy, damaging our bodies and our brains.

> Katie grew up in household where her mother enforced a strict low-fat diet. Later in life, when her mother contracted Alzheimer's and, in conjunction with research on brain health, she discovered that an

overemphasis on low fat can be dangerous. Nutrients are carried to the brain by fat, and a large percentage of the brain is made up of fat. It is more about the type of fat to choose or restrict. Katie now joyfully eats peanuts on the airplane instead of pretzels, and has added avocado and other sources of healthy fat to her diet while still being cautious of excessive animal fats.

4. **Eat high-quality protein.** High-quality protein helps balance your blood sugar, boosts concentration, and provides the necessary building blocks for the rest of your brain. It also provides the amino acids that are used to form neurotransmitters and support structures in neurons.[15] Great sources of protein include fish, skinless turkey or chicken, beans, raw nuts, low-fat or nonfat dairy, and higher-protein vegetables such as broccoli and spinach.

5. **Focus on complex carbohydrates.** Complex carbohydrates keep your blood sugar balanced because they take longer to metabolize. Think of low-glycemic, high-fiber carbohydrates. *Low-glycemic* refers to carbohydrates that do not rapidly raise your blood sugar. Fiber is essential to keep your digestive tract moving. Examples of low-glycemic, high-fiber foods are whole grains, fresh vegetables, many fruits, and beans.

    Low blood-sugar levels are associated with lower overall brain activity. Low brain activity means more cravings and more bad decisions. Simple carbohydrates or high-sugar, high-fat foods spike your blood glucose and then drop it (crash!), harming your brain and your body. They also work on the addiction centers of your brain. This is why you should avoid highly refined food, white bread, and other high-glycemic foods. If you wonder about something you are eating, you can easily go online to see where different foods fit on the glycemic index.

Eating in a balanced way with complex carbohydrates and lean proteins in consistent intervals, four to six times during the day, keeps your blood sugar moderated and provides you with constant energy throughout your day. If you need help in this area, find some healthy, non-sugary snacks (like nuts or fruit) and keep them with you. When you have a desire to eat, eat those.

6. **Eat from the rainbow.** You may have heard of the rainbow diet, which means that you eat a wide variety of colorful, natural foods. (Jelly beans do not count.) What this does is ensure that we get the full range of micronutrients and phytochemicals, like antioxidants, that our brains and bodies need. When you prepare your meal, think in colors like blue (blueberries), red (pomegranates, strawberries, raspberries, cherries, red bell peppers, and tomatoes), yellow (squash, yellow bell peppers, peaches, and bananas), orange (oranges, tangerines, and yams), green (spinach, broccoli, and peas), purple (plums, eggplant), and so on.

7. **Be wise with supplements.** There are a lot of wild claims for some supplements out there, and your nutrition is best derived from whole, natural foods. However, there are also some supplements that are pretty well researched and may have a beneficial impact on the brain, including fish oil (high in omega-3 fatty acids) and vitamin D. Studies are ongoing, so when it comes to supplements, do your homework and always consult your doctor.

The idea is that when you fuel your brain with the right amount of whole, natural foods in regular intervals throughout the day, you provide your brain and body with a steady supply of glucose and other nutrients that help you function at your best. As Colin Campbell, author of one well-respected book, *The China Study*, states:

> Our bodies have evolved with this infinitely complex network of reactions in order to derive maximal benefit from whole foods, as they appear in nature. The misguided may trumpet the virtues of one specific nutrient or chemical, but this thinking is too simplistic. Our bodies have learned how to benefit from the chemicals in food as they are packaged together, discarding some and using others as they see fit.[16]

When we eat this way, we find that we do not need sugar hits and other artificial stimulants to get through the day. We feel better and more energetic, our moods are more positive, and our brains work better.

Does what you eat consist primarily of high-quality, whole, natural foods? Do you eat at regular intervals (four to six times) during the day, or do you go long stretches without eating at all? Do you rely on caffeine, simple sugars, or other stimulants to get you through the day? Are there a few things you could do now to make your diet more friendly to your brain?

DRIVER 3: SLEEP

On May 31, 2009, Air France Flight 447 was carrying 228 people from Brazil to France when it crashed into the Atlantic Ocean, killing everyone on board. It was one of the deadliest accidents in aviation history. Although there were multiple factors that contributed to the accident, it became apparent that the pilots' and crew's lack of sleep was likely a contributing factor.[17]

The Centers for Disease Control and Prevention recently called sleep deprivation a public health epidemic, citing studies showing that:

> Sleep is increasingly recognized as important to public health, with sleep insufficiency linked to motor vehicle crashes, industrial disasters, and medical and other occupational errors.... Persons experiencing sleep insufficiency are also more likely to suffer from chronic diseases such as hypertension, diabetes, depression, and obesity, as well as from cancer, increased mortality, and reduced quality of life and productivity.[18]

There is plenty of research about the medical impact of sleep deprivation, but let's consider it from a brain-performance perspective. As Dr. Liz Joy states:

> Sleep promotes renewal. It's when we consolidate our memories. It's what allows us to remember things from day to day. So if you have an important meeting coming up, you will want to process that information while you're sleeping so that you can actually use it the next day. That's one of the things that sleep does for us. Sleep improves your memories. It improves your cognition. It allows you to be a thinking person.[19]

One study indicated that individuals who had gone seventeen to nineteen hours without sleep performed like someone with a

.05 percent blood-alcohol level, with response times up to 50 percent slower for some tests. After longer periods without sleep, their performance grew even worse, matching a .1 percent blood-alcohol level.[20] In terms of performance, this means that showing up to work sleep-deprived is like showing up drunk.

The real question is how do we want to feel throughout the day? Do we want to go through our day foggy-headed, unsure of our performance? Or would we rather feel rested and ready, knowing that we are operating at our best? Assuming we want to operate at our best, the question then becomes, "How do we get better sleep?"

If you want better sleep, try the following suggestions:

1. **Exercise.** The Move and Sleep drivers are inextricably connected. It turns out that exercise is a great way to sleep well. When you exercise regularly, your body needs better recovery, so it naturally goes into a deeper and more restful sleep.[21] However, many people find that exercising right before bedtime wakes them up, so paying attention to when you exercise is also important. The key is what works for you.

2. **Turn off your devices.** If you spend time watching television or checking email right before bed, the light that goes into your eyes can cue the brain that it is daytime instead of nighttime. "Any light at night can be disruptive, researchers say, but in recent years studies have zeroed in on the particularly potent "blue light" emitted abundantly from the energy-efficient screens of smartphones and computers....."[22] According to Harvard Medical School sleep researcher Steven Lockley, "Blue light preferentially

alerts the brain, suppresses the melatonin, and shifts your body clock all at the same time."[23] Also, whether your devices are on or not, keeping them right by you all night can be a source of mental distraction and stress as you wonder what is popping up in your social media or the company email. Some people find it helps to put all their devices in another room to physically remind them that work is done and now it is time to sleep.

3. **Watch out for caffeine and alcohol.** When you drink a cup of coffee, it takes fifteen to thirty minutes to start having a stimulating effect on the brain, with peak blood levels being reached in about an hour. It then takes three to seven hours for that to be reduced by half, depending on your age, weight, and tolerance for caffeine. So as William C. Dement, author of the bestselling *The Promise of Sleep*, states, "Don't think you can have a cup or two of coffee or tea at 6:00 p.m. and have all the caffeine out of your system by the time you go to bed at 11:00."[24] Consuming alcohol close to bedtime can also affect your ability to sleep, as can eating a heavy meal. Again, the specific effect on you and your body can depend on a number of factors. The key is to try some variation and watch what happens so that you can make the appropriate changes to help you get a better night's rest.

4. **Set up a great sleep environment.** Individual factors like temperature, the firmness or softness of your mattress, the feel of your bed sheets, the noise level, and particularly the amount of light in the room can have a significant impact on the quality of your sleep. Take some time to experiment and set up a room that supports your ability to sleep. This may take some negotiation if someone sleeps with you, but

if you approach it right, you can both probably come out ahead.

5. **Get technical.** For the intrepid, there are a number of simple, wearable devices out on the market that can measure your sleep. (Think a bracelet or wristwatch.) If you really want a window into your sleep behavior, investing in something like this might be helpful.

In the end, these things work if they actually improve your sleep. Here's a summary checklist of indicators from *The Promise of Sleep* that can help you assess your likelihood of getting a good night's rest: [25]

- Do you carefully avoid caffeinated drinks in the evening?
- Do you typically schedule your evening meal at least three hours before you go to bed?
- Do you have a regular bedtime, which you follow with rare exceptions?
- Do you have a bedtime ritual such as a hot bath and perhaps reading a few pages, relaxing while drowsiness sneaks up on you?
- Is your bedroom generally a quiet place all night long?
- Is the temperature of your bedroom just right?
- Do you think of your bed, particularly your mattress and pillows, as the most comfortable place in the world?
- Are the bedclothes (blankets, quilts, comforters) exactly right for you?

As always, these great behaviors are right in the middle of Q2— things that require a conscious choice to schedule and implement.

And like all Q2 activities, they offer a disproportionate return on that investment. You need to ask yourself, "What is it worth to me to go through the day feeling clear-headed, calm, rested, and functioning at my best?" That is the return on a mindfully chosen pattern of sleep. As William Dement states, "If you are serious about your health, nutrition, and fitness, you need to be serious about your sleep."[26]

DRIVER 4: RELAX

We often tend to think of being extraordinarily productive as being on and constantly going all the time. In reality, nothing is further from the truth. High performers realize the importance of conscious, regular recovery after periods of high exertion. Driver 4: Relax has to do with how we manage that recovery, as well as how we handle stress during those moments when we are on. When we do this well, we keep our energy high.

VALUING RECOVERY

In the world of high-performance competitive sports, the quality of athletic recovery is receiving a lot of attention. For many years, the emphasis has been on avoiding overtraining, which happens when athletes work out, train, and perform too much or for too long. When this happens, the body loses its energy and the athlete loses his or her spirit. This results in burnout that is not much different than overwork in the corporate setting or being overstressed in life.

The shift in thinking over the past several years in the athletic field is that, rather than focusing on the problem of overtraining, a more helpful approach may be to focus on the problem of under-recovery.[27] The reason the shift is important is that it changes the way that you solve the problem. The goal in both cases is the same: to keep actual performance high.

If the problem is perceived as overtraining, you might simply try to solve it by lightening the training load, just as you might try to slow down at work a bit if you are feeling too stressed.

However, if you view the problem as under-recovery, you would instead be very diligent and programmed about integrating activities into your life that charge you up and help balance the load of work in your life. As one researcher states, "Reducing the training load is not necessarily the answer to avoiding overtraining."[28]

The upside of this is that you must pay as much attention to your recovery as you do your training [or work!].[29] This is often difficult, because:

> . . . we tend to be consumed by the perspective that the thing we want to happen—getting stronger, faster, fitter—is happening only when we're working on it, exerting some kind of control. We aren't used to the idea that letting go, resting, relaxing control can be as important to healing, recovery, and strengthening as they are.[30]

Because of this tendency, "attention to recovery may even take more discipline than training."[31]

For our purposes, this means we must be very conscious about identifying the Q2 activities that truly renew us and help us restore our energy, then be very disciplined—without guilt or shame—about getting those activities into our lives.

Remember our discussion of the Time Matrix in Choice 1, where people often bashfully say that they need a little Q4 time?

What people really mean by this is that they need time for relaxing but, for some perverse reason, they assume it is the wrong thing to do because they think it is not productive. In reality, Q2 relaxing or recovery activities are vital to our productivity. They are Big Rocks that affect our performance as powerfully as time spent working directly on a particular task or project.

> Journalist Matt Richtel joined a group of scientists who experimented on themselves by totally disconnecting for several days. "They wanted to take a look at what was happening to their brain and their perspectives—and by extension, ours—as they got off the grid."
>
> They took a raft trip down the San Juan River in southern Utah, one of the most remote places in North America. They had one unbreakable rule: no mobile phones and no Internet. "The reason why I say the rule was not breakable? There was no cell-phone coverage. There was no Internet. Right after we launched our rafts, one of the scientists said it's the end of civilization, by which he meant your cell phone will no longer work."
>
> At the end of three days, the group noticed something happening to themselves. They called it the three-day effect. "You start to feel more relaxed. Maybe you sleep a little better. . . . Maybe you wait a little longer before answering a question. Maybe you don't feel in a rush to do anything. Your sense of urgency fades."
>
> The scientists came away from the experiment with the unequivocal conclusion that downtime was essential for brain health.[32]

Recovery strategies are as unique as the individual, and sometimes the right recovery strategy is to reduce the load of work, or even take some significant time off. Recovery and relaxation might also be as simple as a fifteen-minute break to change your surroundings. Many organizations have gyms or quiet areas where you can go and chill out for a bit. One person we know, who has a small team and not much office space, has dedicated one office for a quiet place where people can go, no questions asked, to rest their brains and recharge before returning to work.

According to an article from *The New York Times,* "A growing body of evidence shows that taking regular breaks from mental tasks improves productivity and creativity—and that skipping breaks can lead to stress and exhaustion."[33]

When you have a balanced approach, in which recovery activities are consistently woven into your life, you will find that you have a sustainable pattern of both work and recovery that can keep you going in an energetic and motivated way over the long term.

Here are some strategies that may be helpful. Look them over and see if you find any that may be renewing for you:

1. A quiet break after completing some important work task
2. Actively pursuing a hobby
3. Watching an inspiring movie or your favorite TV show
4. Visiting a couple of websites you find interesting
5. Talking to a friend
6. Taking a walk
7. Listening to music
8. Getting a massage
9. Power naps
10. Exercise
11. Going out with friends
12. Going for a hike in the mountains

13. Meditation

14. Community service

15. Playing games

16. Yoga

17. Calling a friend

18. Being with family

19. Spiritual practices or worship

20. Laughing

21. Working in the yard

22. Switching projects at work

23. Reading a good book

24. Taking some deep breaths

The bottom line is that these activities are just as important as anything else you are doing, and are right in the middle of Q2! However, because they are in Q2, that means they are unlikely to happen by themselves. This means you have to be conscious about choosing and implementing your recovery strategies—just as you will need to be for each one of the 5 Energy Drivers!

KEEPING CALM WHEN THE HEAT IS ON

The other aspect of Energy Driver 4 is how you handle your stress in those moments when you are working and not in recovery.

If you've seen the movie *Gravity,* you've seen a great example of how two people handle a stressful situation very differently. In the film, which won seven Academy Awards, Sandra Bullock and George Clooney play two astronauts who are stranded in space when debris strikes and destroys their space shuttle.

As the story unfolds, Commander Matt Kowalski (played by Clooney) is a veteran astronaut, and it shows. As the debris strikes the shuttle, Kowalski handles the crisis with calm, focused attention and is in full command of himself. He spends his energy trying to calm Dr. Ryan Stone (played by Bullock), who is in space for the first time. Even before the accident, she is tense and nervous and, when the strike occurs, her body goes into a full stress response, with rapid breathing and mental overload impairing her ability to speak or act in any way that is helpful. It is not until she gets control of her own body that she is able to start acting in a positive way to deal with the disaster. Throughout the movie, Dr. Stone finds her own courage and internal strength to take the steps that get her safely home.

While most of us are unlikely to face a crisis that dramatic, isn't it interesting how people can respond to challenging situations so differently? It's always impressive when someone comes into a stressful circumstance and, with a calm and centered approach, makes good decisions and carries them out with confidence.

While some may come to this state more naturally than others, the good news is that this is a learnable skill, and the better you are at it, the more clearly you can see to make good decisions when the heat is on, allowing you to focus your energy where it matters instead of wasting it on dealing with stress.

The stress response that paralyzed Dr. Stone has its roots in— you guessed it—the Reactive Brain. When we face situations we regard as stressful, a whole flood of chemicals is unleashed within milliseconds to mobilize our body for action. This can have three results: fight (ready for combat), flight (ready to run), or, in some cases, freeze (not ready to do anything at all). The same stress hormones trigger all three of these outcomes: cortisol and adrenaline.

The body's stress response can be very helpful when we need to mobilize our body to respond to a short-term threat. What is not helpful is that all this biology decreases the functioning of our Thinking Brain. The result is that, when we are stressed, we do not think clearly or make good decisions. Additionally, when we live in a prolonged state of stress, it has all sorts of physical and mental effects, including immune-system disorders and cardiovascular disease, as well as anxiety and depression.

In 1975, Herbert Benson's pioneering book *The Relaxation Response* put forth the idea that we could train our brains away from the stress response and replace it with what he called the "relaxation response."[34] In the decades that have followed, a bevy of scientific research has backed up his claim, and the mechanics are quite well known; we just have to learn how to do it. As Dan Harris stated in his recent book *10% Happier,* "The brain, the organ of experience, through which our entire lives are led, can be trained. Happiness is a skill."[35]

There are a number of techniques that can help you develop a relaxation response, but they all come down to finding a mental and physical routine that helps you pause and think differently so that your Reactive Brain simmers down and you can return to your Thinking Brain. As you practice these routines, your brain becomes better at them, and you actually can change the way you respond to stress. Whatever you use is fine, as long as it works and you practice it.

Here are a few of the most broadly validated techniques:

- **Distancing.** Take a picture of the stressful situation or person in your mind and move that image far away so that the individual or setting is small. Your brain is wired to respond to large, in-your-face things as a threat. By minimizing the image, it helps the brain not get so revved up. Additionally, you can imagine that person talking in a small chipmunk voice, which also minimizes the sense of threat and adds a bit of humor as well.

- **Reframing.** When you view something as a threat or an un-welcome source of stress, your brain responds accordingly. When you reframe or reappraise it as a positive challenge that you are anxious to take on, your brain responds in a more helpful way.[36] Seeing challenges as essential stepping-stones to achieving important Q2 Goals can also give you motivation.

- **Taking a Deep Breath.** Taking a deep breath and counting to ten changes both your physiology and brain chemistry. The additional oxygen helps, and can provide you the necessary pause for your Reactive Brain to back off while your Thinking Brain takes over.

- **Meditating.** The research is abundant on the stress-relieving benefits of regular meditation. Not only does it help you reach more relaxed states while meditating; it actually can reset your normal state so that you are calmer throughout the day and don't get so riled up under pressure. This is rewiring your brain at its best, and you don't have to wear a robe and go for Nirvana to make it happen. It's simply a technique you can use to push different chemical buttons in your brain, leaving you in a better place to deal with the stresses of life.

Do you have an effective relaxation technique? If you do, keep going! If you don't, pick one of the techniques above that seems like it might work, or find another one that is appealing to you. The practiced ability to pause your Reactive Brain and consciously access your Thinking Brain is central to the good decisions that allow for extraordinary productivity.

CHALLENGE THE ANTs

One final technique we will share comes from Dr. Daniel Amen. Here's what he says:

> Stress is probably the biggest robber of mental energy and, in my experience, the number-one cause of stress is the negative thoughts running around your head. I actually call them ANTs: automatic negative thoughts—the thoughts that come into your mind automatically and ruin your day.
>
> So whenever you feel sad, mad, nervous, or out of control, write down your automatic negative thoughts. Write down the negative thoughts and then ask yourself if they're true. Writing them down gets them out of your head. Challenging them uses the front, thoughtful part of your brain to get rid of them.[37]

Writing things down is a very powerful technique and, again, you can see the pattern: turn off your Reactive Brain and engage your Thinking Brain. In reality, most things aren't as bad as your Reactive Brain makes them out to be. And if they are, at least you are in a better place to deal with them.

A FINAL THOUGHT ON Q2 PLANNING AND STRESS

In the end, one of the best things you can do to remove stress on a day-to-day basis is to become good at the Q2 Planning systems of Choice 3: Schedule the Big Rocks, Don't Sort Gravel. Using a

Master Task List to capture everything important, using Q2 Time Zones to create order and structure around your priorities, and practicing Weekly and Daily Q2 Planning based on your deepest desires and motivations will give you peace of mind and a sense of integrity that will remove so much of the self-imposed stress you carry during the day. These techniques will help you navigate the external pressures of life with confidence that everything is in order and your most important priorities are taken care of.

DRIVER 5: CONNECT

We may not think of relationships as a way to increase mental energy, but they are. Not only is the brain wired for movement, but it is also an inherently social organ. It is designed to help us interact with others and form strong communal relationships that contribute to our survival and well-being.

One example of how this works is the hormone *oxytocin,* which acts as a neuromodulator in the brain. Oxytocin increases feelings of trust, bonding, and closeness with others, and can reduce feelings of fear and stress. It is a feel-good and essential hormone that is fostered in healthy relationships and also helps us get along well with those around us.[38]

When we have close, mutually nurturing relationships in our lives, we have a treasured source of energy and well-being. According to a Harvard Medical School publication:

Dozens of studies have shown that people who have satisfying relationships with family, friends, and their community are happier, have fewer health problems, and live longer. Conversely, a relative lack of social ties is associated with depression and later-life cognitive decline, as well as with increased mortality. One study, which examined data from more than 309,000 people, found that lack of strong relationships increased the risk of premature death from all causes by 50%—an effect on mortality risk roughly comparable to smoking up to 15 cigarettes a day.[39]

Additionally, research shows that healthy human relationships can actually have a healing effect on the body. In contrast, social pain is interpreted in the same way as physical pain (like a broken leg) in the brain.[40]

This kind of benefit is something that happens one-on-one, in real interactions, rather than online. In one study that looked at Internet use and its effect on relationships, researchers found that cyberspace relationships do not provide the kind of psychological support and happiness derived from real-life contact. This is because, as Robert Kraut, the study's author, suggested, "there are more cases where you're building shallow relationships, leading to an overall decline in feeling of connection to other people."[41]

Finally, as another researcher states, "Scientists have had to expand their thinking to grasp the idea that individual neurons or single human brains do not exist in nature. Without mutually stimulating interactions, people and neurons wither and die."[42]

It takes time and commitment to create these relationships and, if we do not make them a priority, we can easily miss out on the health, vitality, strength, and energy that come from authentic relationships with other people. Yet, so often in our busy lives, these things fall to the bottom of our lists.

Lisa was in her forties when she had a moment of significant reappraisal in her life. She had been working hard on a long and challenging project and was hit with a significant illness that required her to take several months off from work.

She was a woman who would have said that she took care of herself. She ate in a healthy way, exercised, and loved her work, but this time of sickness literally forced her to think about other aspects of her life for an extended period of time. What she found was both instructive and challenging to her pattern of life.

She realized that because she was engaged in her work, she had created an artificial sense of meaning that obscured some of her deeper needs. The praise and accolades she had been receiving had kept her going. However, sitting at home alone, she became aware that there was a deeper emptiness that had not been filled, and that it had been there for a long time. She said, "I was running on fumes, not fuel. And when I needed the strength that came from those deeper sources, they simply weren't there."

She looked back on decisions she had made in her early thirties, including a career that included a lot of travel. Although she had a number of friends, she had never developed a deep, committed relationship with someone. As she looked toward the future, she asked herself, "Do I want to repeat that decade?"

She also realized that she "had been governed by an artificial flow of life that was defined by tasks and projects rather than minutes and hours. My forced recovery made me aware of minutes and hours in a very real way. When you are in the task mode, days and weeks go by and you have no concept of time. Entire seasons pass you by and you are out of touch with the natural rhythm of the world. I said to myself, 'Where have I been? Why have I been missing this?'"

As a result, Lisa began to invest in creating deeper relationships and to consciously connect with the fundamental rhythms of nature. "Good work is important," she said, "but it doesn't fill you in the same way as a meaningful relationship with another human being. The ability to love and be loved is so enriching and rewarding. That need was always there, but it was hidden and I wasn't really aware of it. When those deeper wells are filled, I have greater perspective and strength. I can make better decisions about my work and my life. I feel complete."

This story highlights the value of balance among all 5 Energy Drivers. Even if you are doing well on some of them, ignoring other aspects of your self can drain you of your resources and deeper wells of energy. We are whole people, and any aspect of ourselves that gets passed over or ignored will eventually come back to catch us.

But connecting in this way takes conscious Q2 effort in today's world. As Dr. Ed Hallowell states:

The human moment is disappearing from modern life. It's being replaced by the electronic moment. A human moment requires two elements: number one, physical presence and number two, attention. So just being together doesn't make a human moment. You can sit next to someone on an airplane and not have a human moment at all. You have to really focus. That means disengaged from your laptop. That means get off your cell phone. You cannot multitask and have a productive human moment. You have to put it all aside, make eye contact, and connect with that other person: listen, relax, don't be in a hurry. . . . People are starved from connecting in this way because it so rarely happens. And if you can make it your business to be able to put everything down, really connect with that other person, it's like someone who's been on a desert discovering an oasis: ah, at last![43]

Consider your own relationships and the quality of your connection with those people. Are there some relationships where the connection is not what it could be? Are you neglecting some key relationships in your life? Are there some Q2 things you can do to invest in building those relationships?

SOLVING THE ENERGY CRISIS

Each of these 5 Energy Drivers is powerful in its own right. If you invest time in even one of them, you will get a quick and clear benefit. However, the real power comes when you have a regular pattern of life that honors all 5 Energy Drivers. When you have a healthy pattern of movement, eating, sleeping, relaxing, and connecting, you are strengthening yourself as a complete human being. In this setting, the 5 Energy Drivers work together to fuel your mind and body so that you can make better decisions, focus your attention and energy, and feel accomplished at the end of every day.

When you make Q2 investments in yourself, you have more to give to the purposes and goals you care about, you feel better about yourself and your mind is clearer and more receptive to the great things that are possible. Getting good at Choice 5: Fuel Your Fire, Don't Burn Out is the foundation of your ability to implement all the other choices and gives you the energy to do everything else.

SIMPLE WAYS TO GET STARTED

You can begin applying the principles and practices of Choice 5: Fuel Your Fire, Don't Burn Out by taking any of the following simple actions. Pick the ones that work best for you.

- Pick one way to increase your movement at work and consciously do it at least once each day this week. Put a check mark on your calendar when you do it so that your brain can congratulate you!
- Buy some healthy snacks (fruits, vegetables, etc.) and put them in your desk so you have something healthy to munch on.
- Go to bed fifteen minutes earlier than you normally do.
- Plan something fun this week that helps you relax.
- Spend a little extra time strengthening a key relationship in your life.

TO SUM UP

- Your brain is your number-one asset in a knowledge-work world.
- Being conscious and intentional throughout the day takes a lot of energy.
- There are two sources of energy: a clear and motivating purpose and a healthy physical body.
- There are 5 Energy Drivers: Move, Eat, Sleep, Relax, and Connect.
- When you make regular investments in these 5 Energy Drivers, you create a pattern of life that fuels your fire and keeps you from burning out.

YOUR EXTRAORDINARY LIFE

How we spend our days is, of course, how we spend our lives.

—Annie Dillard

When the alarm went off next to Kiva's bed, she instinctively reached for her phone. (It was a hard habit to break!) However, this time, on her nightstand she felt her new shoes and yoga outfit. "Oh, yeah," she thought, "today is the day I start!"

She had consciously put her phone in another room last night and put her yoga gear on her nightstand to help her remember her commitment to exercise this morning. Knowing that she couldn't escape the accountability she had set up with Kellie at work, she grabbed her gear and walked out to the television to start her new program.

It took a few minutes to get going, but after thirty minutes of movement and stretching, she felt energized and ready for the day.

Smiling, she walked to the fridge and grabbed a yogurt and

some other healthy stuff, and sat down to look at her coming day. There were a couple of important things she had planned to do today at work and she wanted to make sure that she would devote the time to focus on them. As she reviewed her calendar and tasks, the thought came to her that she could use some additional data for her upcoming project review and, if she started on it today, she would have it ready by the meeting. She quickly rearranged her schedule and blocked out an hour to work on it as well. Satisfied that her highest priorities for the day were in place, she finished getting ready for the day.

While waiting for the train to arrive, she texted Kellie that she had completed her yoga routine. "Me too! :)" Kellie texted back. Who knew that Kellie had a thing for yoga? Kiva was glad for the support as she worked to get this new routine in place.

Kiva used the train ride into town to review some of her project-status reports and check the emails her rules had marked critical. Then, for the final ten minutes of the ride, she closed the laptop and looked around. The sun had come up over the trees a few minutes ago, and it looked like it was going to be a nice day. "Maybe I could do something outdoors this weekend?" She made a task to call her brother, who lived nearby, to see if he had anything planned.

As she walked into the office, her peaceful and calm demeanor was immediately assaulted by . . . Karl! "Seriously?" she thought, "is that guy everywhere! Okay, Karl. Let's see what you've got." As she listened to Karl, she realized that most of the information he was asking her for was available on the system, if only he would take the time to look. "Karl," she said, "I would like to help you, but honestly, this is information you should be able to find. Let's go over to Shareese in accounting, and she can show you how to pull this data from the system. That's what her job is, and I know she'd be glad to help you." After walking Karl over to Shareese and telling her what Karl needed, Kiva headed back to her desk.

Throughout the day, she was able to keep pretty much to her schedule. There was one critical meeting that came up, but she was able to make a change and accommodate it. Another meeting had come up as well, but as she paused and thought about it, it was not that important to attend, so she declined.

She was glad she had made some time today to gather data for the upcoming project review because, as she looked at it, she realized there were some vital questions that would likely come up and that she would need to respond to. She knew that others would be involved as well, so she checked their availability and set up a meeting with John and Livya, the two relevant members of her team, for the following day. She quickly typed in the body of the invite what the meeting was for, and attached the data she had already collected so that they could review it ahead of time.

At the end of the day, she took a few moments to review what she had accomplished, capture some key information in her notes, transfer some tasks, and close out the day on her calendar.

As she walked out of the office, she felt lighter than she anticipated. She realized that even though there were a few Q1s that had come her way, she had accomplished the important things she set out to do and that the rest were in their proper place. She realized that she hadn't altered her day much, but had done a few things that had made her day much more productive and fulfilling. As her mind reveled in that realization, a smile crossed her face and she thought about calling her brother. "It's been a while," she thought. "It will be wonderful to spend some quality time with him. I wonder what he's up to?"

More than anything, extraordinary productivity is a question of being conscious in the moment. And it doesn't take much to change the equation. It's taking small steps each day to cultivate this habit in our lives. It's being aware of our surroundings, the people we work with, and the opportunities for high-value decisions about where we spend our time, attention, and energy.

When we live our days this way, we find they are much more rewarding and fulfilling. We know that we have been involved in things that matter and have done them well. We can feel accomplished at the end of every day. And in the end, we may be surprised to find out that a series of extraordinary days has given us an extraordinary life!

SPECIAL SECTION: BEING A Q2 LEADER

WHAT LEADERS CAN DO

Leadership is a choice, not a position.

—Stephen R. Covey

A culture is particularly sensitive to the actions of its leaders. Almost by definition, they have a disproportionate impact on how a culture feels and what people do. But leadership is not just a position; in fact, some of the most powerful leaders in the world held no real formal position of power (think Mother Teresa or Gandhi). By this definition, leadership is a choice, not a position.

When we think of leaders, we think of anyone who is willing to involve others to make a change. You can be a leader in your team or organization; you can be a leader in your family or community. Anyone who wants to make things better and take the actions required can be a leader.

The suggestions here are ideas about how you can exercise

leadership in each of the 5 Choices to create a Q2 culture among those you work with. They show how the principles of each choice can be applied in different circumstances to create more productive outcomes. Many of these suggestions are targeted to those who have formal authority. Others can be acted on regardless of your position. In every case, they require your commitment to consciously model the behaviors of the 5 Choices to others.

If you are a senior-level leader and would like to develop a Q2 culture throughout your organization in a formal way, see the next chapter, "Building a Q2 Culture in Your Organization." However, this chapter is for everyone who is willing to lead and make a difference in their own setting. Simply review the ideas that follow, see which ones apply, and make a commitment to implement them one at a time.

CHOICE 1: ACT ON THE IMPORTANT, DON'T REACT TO THE URGENT

- **Share your commitment to a Q2 culture with those around you.** Be explicit about what you are trying to achieve and how it can help everyone feel more accomplished at the end of every day. By making a public commitment, you are saying, "This is important. I am willing to be accountable for this."

- **Teach the Time Matrix and link it to business results.** Take time in team meetings or in other settings to teach people about the Time Matrix and the ROI of acting in Q2. Make posters of the Time Matrix and hang them where people can see them. Put your team or corporate goals in Q2 so that they know what the priorities are and why Q2 matters. When you create a clear business linkage, everyone can make better decisions about where they should be spending their time, attention, and energy. They can also see what's at stake, and see the dangers of distraction or waste. They will realize that Q1 activities, while important, can take away from their collective ability to do quality work on the Q2 Goals. Customize the other quadrants as well, with specific examples of distractions or crises that tend to occur in your team or organization so that people will watch out for them.

- **Have Q2 Conversations with everyone.** Sit down with an individual and help clarify what is in Q2. It could be with your boss (clarifying what is in Q2 for you), but as a leader, you can help others become conscious and intentional about what is important in their role. If you have informal authority, you can do it as a peer or recommend the process as you start projects, establish working relationships, or interact with others. If you are a formal leader, you can make this a part of your leadership coaching and performance reviews. Talk about the organization's critical goals and measures, and talk about how people can better focus on those things in Q2. Ask people what is getting in the way of their ability to focus on those things. Be open and candid. Are people spending enough time on the important things? How can you improve their focus? What could be eliminated? Where possible, be ruthless about getting rid of Q3s and Q4s so that you can build a conscious, healthy, and productive Q2 culture.

- **Use the language of importance in normal conversation.** As a leader, what you say has an impact. Use terms like Q1, Q2, Q3, and Q4; Thinking Brain and Reactive Brain; moment of choice; Pause-Clarify-Decide; and decision, attention, and energy management. Ask whether things are important or merely urgent. Ask people about their results, not just how busy they are. Consciously using the language of importance, instead of the language of busyness, underscores that your culture is about getting important things done.

- **Allow for strategic pauses.** Create an environment where it is safe for people to press the pause button and make good decisions about where they are spending their time, attention, and energy. Allow for tough clarifying questions like: Why are we doing this? How will this contribute to our desired results? Does this have to be done now? Is this a distraction from higher priorities? Should we be doing this at all?

  We are not talking about challenging everything all at once or being reckless about this. People need to use judgment and act wisely. And frankly, there are just some things that need to be done because someone higher up wants it that way. However, as you pick your targets and the culture starts to shift over time, more and more of what people do will be tied to more meaningful results.

- **Create strategic pauses.** You can help your culture learn to pause and make better decisions by doing it yourself in public settings—even better if you are challenging one of your own initiatives! The answers to these questions may be uncomfortable at times, but when people have the capability to challenge their work, then they will also have the opportunity to more fully commit to the things that really will make a difference. When people see you act with integrity to the principles and to the process, you give them permission and encouragement to do the same thing.

- **Help other leaders clearly define Q2.** If you are a leader of leaders, then helping them live the 5 Choices and focus on

Q2 can have a significant impact for them and those they lead. Talk through the key elements of the Q2 Role Statement. What are they focused on? What are their key Q2 Goals? Review what they are doing with the Time Matrix and make sure they are clear as to what is truly important. Challenge them to get rid of or delegate other tasks so that they can make their highest contribution. This can be especially important for new leaders, who may still be trying to do the things that made them successful as individual contributors and are not assigning work or delegating as they should. Help them learn that to be successful in their new role as a leader, they need to focus on different things than they did in the past. The activities that were in Q2 before they became leaders are now different. Their change in role has changed what is in Q2 for them and what they should be focused on. This is true for anybody who is changing roles; they need to redefine what is important in that role and plan to get those things done.

- **Don't put people into Q1.** Lack of preparation on your part can have a devastating impact on the people beneath you. We call this the "click-spin" theory of organizations. Think of a bunch of gears connected together. When the big leader gear rotates and makes a click (some decision, some need for information, etc.), another gear somewhere down in the organization starts spinning rapidly to meet that need. That's okay if you are a formal leader; your job is to make decisions that cause others to do work. However, if you are operating in Q1 because you have not prepared or thought ahead, then that is creating an unnecessary crisis for others. You may have heard the statement, "A lack of preparation on your part does not constitute a crisis on my part." This idea applies to leaders as well. Because you are in a position of power, others may not call you on it, so your ability to be self-aware is vital. Being personally prepared and not abusing your position of power can make a huge difference in your organization.

- **Don't put people into Q3.** The dark side of click-spin is that you can send individuals or entire groups of people off into Q3 distractions pretty easily. Sometimes leaders will, without thinking, wonder out loud about some bit of information, and it becomes someone's project for the next seventy-two hours. If it is important information, then that might be a Q1 or a Q2. But if it is not important, it just became a waste of that person's time. Make sure that you only pursue the important. Apply the filters before you ask someone to do something for you. If it is important, go ahead and ask with confidence. That's why you are a leader. If it is not, ditch it.

- **Stop the assumptions.** Be very aware that direct reports tend to assume everything you ask for is needed now. That's because it has been the standard operating procedure for so long. Even if you had not intended for a particular project to start for six months, you might find that someone rapidly started spinning by default. Be very clear about your expectations to break this pattern.

- **Create positive rituals.** Just as families have traditions around holidays, vacations, and so on, organizations can establish traditions or rituals around how well they focus on their Q2 priorities. Some things just evolve that are unique to a particular culture, while others are consciously put in place. In one organization, a leader might establish a Q3 graveyard, where every time a significant distraction is eliminated, it can be posted on the wall with a headstone and recognition for the person who got rid of it. In another culture, a leader might honor projects that are completed on time, with quality, and without a big rush at the end (instead of celebrating the Q1-crisis hero who rushed in at the last minute to save everything). What you do is up to you, but be on the lookout for things you can set up as traditions that reinforce a Q2 focus.

- **Reward Q2.** Rewarding heroics is part of our corporate DNA. An emergency well handled gets the gold star at the monthly employee meeting. If we are not careful, we can be encouraging a Q1 culture. Nurture the higher-return Q2 culture by seeking out those accomplishments that get at root causes and prevent Q1s or projects that are completed on time and on budget without a rush, or teams that generate a great idea with an impressive future return. This is an effective way to move your culture into its Thinking Brain.

CHOICE 2: GO FOR EXTRAORDINARY, DON'T SETTLE FOR ORDINARY

- **Share your own leadership Q2 Role Statements and Q2 Goals with others.** Where you choose to deploy your own energy as a leader is vital. Let people in on your personal priorities as a leader. Tell them what you are trying to accomplish. If some parts are too personal, that's fine. Share what you can. By articulating your priorities to your team, it helps them calibrate their own efforts to make these things happen. As a leader, you cannot (and should not) try to do everything. Pick the two or three most important things you want to accomplish and organize around them. Eliminate or delegate other tasks. Be vocal about the contributions you need to make and help others understand the purpose for your focus. They will appreciate the clarity and focus for their own jobs. They may even have good ideas to help you better do the things you are focused on.

- **Ask others to define Q2 Role Statements and Q2 Goals.** If you are a formal leader and can do this, ask people on your team to come up with the contribution they want to make in their role and share it with you. The conversations you have can be both illuminating and motivating. You can apply this principle to teams as well as individuals. Imagine a project team that kicks off the project with a short, motivating statement about the contribution of that project to the organization and how it links to the organization's goals. You can make this kind of thinking standard in your organization.

- **Use the From X to Y by When formula when setting organizational goals.** Build on the current brain science when formulating your goals. The specificity of this formula will help you and everyone else make better decisions around where to spend your time, attention, and energy.

CHOICE 3: SCHEDULE THE BIG ROCKS, DON'T SORT GRAVEL

- **Create organizational Q2 Time Zones.** As a leader, you should be involving others and looking months, quarters, and even years into the future. If you are not, then you are not doing your job. By looking as far ahead as possible, and by blocking out key events or patterns (like the quarterly close, or fall product launches), you are allowing members of your organization to prepare to do their work well and work in Q2. You can build processes around repeating events so that you can get better at them. You are also preventing self-inflicted crises that can throw your entire organization into Q1. Some organizations even block out regular patterns of thinking time or innovating time.

- **Practice Q2 Planning with your leadership team.** There is a big difference between a typical team scheduling meeting and a Q2 Planning meeting. A scheduling meeting is characterized by sorting short-term gravel. A Q2 Planning meeting comes from your longer-term contributions and important Q2 Goals. It's about asking what the key activities are that will help you achieve your important organizational results and putting those things in first. Organizations have a collective Reactive Brain and a Thinking Brain. Q2 Planning helps your team get into its Thinking Brain and schedule what is important instead of what is merely urgent.

- **Do Q2 daily huddles.** In some settings, daily team meetings are essential. For example, in agile software-development environments, teams will often have a daily stand-up meeting to determine what is most important for that day, and remove obstacles to progress. This can be similar to the Daily Q2 Planning individuals do, particularly when team members are focused on accomplishing what is important, removing distractions, and preventing problems that could cause a crisis later on. The principles of Q2 Planning can apply in a variety of settings once you have the Q2 mindset and language.

- **Get good at what you do a lot of.** Spending Q2 time with your team to set up a good process around your most vital and repeatable work can help everyone in your organization stay focused in Q2. It avoids waste and rework, and gives people a firm foundation to stand on. As the process guru W. Edwards Deming said, "If you can't describe what you are doing as a process, you don't know what you're doing."[1]

CHOICE 4: RULE YOUR TECHNOLOGY, DON'T LET IT RULE YOU

- **Create an organizational Q2 manifesto.** As a leader, take the initiative to set clear guidelines and protocols about how to handle email, texts, and so forth. Help your team know how to prioritize communications from you and those they send to others. Set some common guidelines and rules. Let them know when they can safely unplug. When expectations and protocols are clear, stress goes down and people are free to focus their creativity and attention on the most important things.

- **Get your technology right.** As a leader, you may have influence over the systems and technologies used by your organization. Pick technologies that help people organize the Core 4. Get good spam filters in place. Examine firewalls and authentication policies to ensure everyone's ability to organize their Core 4 across devices. It is a war for your people's attention, and you don't want unwanted or unnecessary distractions and barriers keeping people from doing their jobs well. Give them the necessary tools and policies to make critical information available when and where they need it.

- **Teach the Q2 Process Map and hang it on the wall.** Make sure people understand the flow of the map and are skilled at the 3 Master Moves. If your people understand this map, and have the technology and skills to support it, they will be fully armed to win the daily war against the digital incoming. Have regular reviews of the map, and ask people about the status of their rules and whether the protocols you have in place help them turn things into what they are and access their Core 4 easily.

CHOICE 5: FUEL YOUR FIRE, DON'T BURN OUT

- **Take care of yourself.** Leadership is some of the hardest knowledge work there is. Being an effective organizational leader takes all kinds of mental and emotional energy. As a leader, no one deserves the benefits of a Q2 lifestyle more than you do. The principles of the 5 Choices will not only help you be an effective leader of your organization; they may also keep you loving your job and avoiding your own burnout. Start by taking care of yourself and living the 5 Choices personally. Take time to exercise, eat brain-healthy food, sleep well, have regular Q2 renewal and relaxation, and strengthen key relationships. You will be a better leader if you do.
- **Provide healthy food options.** This one is sure to be a hit at the office. Everybody loves food, and if you start providing healthy options at work, people will not only thank you for it, they may cheer. When you see people alert and working rather than in sugar comas during afternoon meetings, you will see that it is money well spent.
- **Create brain breaks.** When you can see that a meeting has gone on too long, recommend that everyone take a brain

break. Get up and walk around. Have standing meetings. Take a moment for humor and fun. These things provide a bit of renewal in your work and enliven the culture. They also make the next round of work that much more effective.

- **Honor vacations.** When people take a vacation, let them go! Try to avoid sending them stuff, texting them, or calling them while they are off. If you let people fully relax, then they will come back to the game ready to go.

- **Encourage an ethos of healthy energy versus tough guy.** Foster an ethos of health and energy in your culture versus the tough guy, work-all-hours hero, make-it-happen culture that we often cultivate to get things done. Sure, there are times we choose to work long hours. That's reality. But if the culture celebrates strung-out, bleary-eyed, I-worked-all-night-again patterns of behavior, you are setting yourself up for crises and, what's worse, you are draining your culture of the creative energy you need to discover the next innovative idea that takes you to the next level or lifts you above the competition. Instead, celebrate people who work hard and get outstanding results without turning themselves into office zombies. Celebrate people who choose to bring their very best energy to the workplace—they are the best employees you have. As a leader, the energy you carry and the way you handle your own health will do a lot to shape the culture in this area.

BUILDING A Q2 CULTURE IN YOUR ORGANIZATION

The most important contribution management needs to make in the 21st century is . . . to increase the productivity of knowledge work and the knowledge worker.[1]

—Peter Drucker

This chapter is for senior-level leaders who have the authority and the will to institutionalize a Q2 culture inside their organization. It is an overview of the process you can use to make this happen, and is built on the process used by FranklinCovey to help clients make significant improvements in their organizational cultures.

YOUR CULTURE IS YOUR ORGANIZATION'S OPERATING SYSTEM

Most of the complex electronic devices you own have an operating system. Your smartphone, for instance, could be run by Apple's iOS, Google's Android, Windows, or some other system, but what operating systems exist for is to make everything else run well.

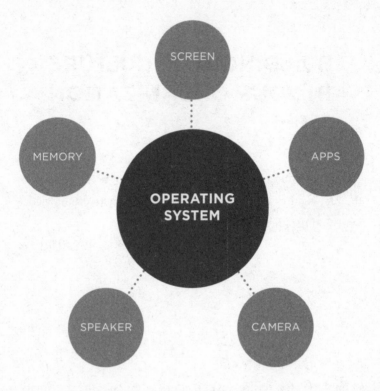

A culture is like an operating system for your organization. If you have a great operating system, then all the things you are trying to do run better. Whether it is achieving revenue goals, accomplishing tasks and projects, serving customers, or improving production processes and systems, if you have a strong operating system, things just work better. If you have a corrupt or dysfunctional operating system, things may not work at all.

When you have a Q2 culture inside your organization, you will find that people:

- **Self-orient** around the highest priorities.
- **Self-select** the activities that will generate the highest return against those priorities.
- **Self-deploy** their finest attention around those activities, while bringing their best selves to work.

When a Q2 culture is in place, the most important things you are trying to achieve just got turbo-charged.

Think about the data we shared at the beginning of this book. We showed the results of a six-year global study of 351,613 respondents, where people indicated that just over 40 percent of their time and energy was being spent on things that were not important to them or to their companies. We also asserted that this was the biggest hidden cost in organizations today, the numbers implying that nearly half of your payroll is being spent on things that don't matter to your strategic goals.

What if you had a culture where people automatically self-oriented around the important things that really made an impact—whether to the bottom line or to other strategic goals you were working on? What if people consistently challenged what they and others were doing to eliminate the things that kept them from being productive? What if people regularly came to work with ample mental and physical energy to accomplish what needed to be done? Most important, what if people regularly chose to invest all their creative talent and energy into their work without holding anything back?

Our data show that within just a few months, organizations can expect to increase the amount of time they spend in Q2 by 24 percent, and in some cases, that number is as high as 35 percent.

However, just like a computer operating system needs an installation process, a Q2 culture does as well. The process we will suggest shows how you can install the 5 Choices in your organization and, within three to six months, expect to see the following measurable and auditable behaviors inside your workplace:

- **Weekly Q2 Conversations in Team Meetings.** Team leaders will be using the Time Matrix regularly in their meetings to help their teams maintain focus on the Big Rocks in Q2 and remove Q3 distractions.
- **Q2 Role Statements and Goals.** Individuals will have created specific statements around the contributions they will make in their work, made specific goals to get there, and validated them with their immediate supervisors. These will be integrated into "Performance" Conversations.
- **Weekly and Daily Q2 Planning.** Individuals will be doing regular Weekly and Daily Q2 Planning with a specific focus on their work goals.
- **Common Technology Protocols.** You will have a common set of email protocols that help people avoid wasting time and use their email more effectively.
- **High-Energy Behaviors.** You will see people exhibiting higher energy and supporting behaviors as measured by the Q2 Energy Index.

You will also see other, more individualized behaviors that come from the 5 Choices and that support a Q2 culture. The auditable behaviors, however, will be spread broadly throughout your organization.

HOW TO INSTALL THE 5 CHOICES IN YOUR CULTURE

The process that follows describes key elements in how we work with organizations to install the 5 Choices as an operating system. You can modify this, as appropriate, if you wish to do this on your own.

1. **Leadership-Team Orientation.** To start, an executive sponsor is chosen as well as a champion team who will be responsible for training the leaders and others inside the organization. During this meeting, which lasts about a half day, the leadership team will learn about the 5 Choices with emphasis on the Time Matrix, then review 5 Choices-related data about their organization and how much time they are currently spending in Q2. They will also discuss what low-hanging opportunities are revealed by the data to either mitigate or eliminate in the other quadrants.

2. **Champion-Team Certification.** Coaches and facilitators inside your organization are certified to facilitate the *5 Choices* Work Session and ensure the rest of the installation and accountability process is successful.

3. **Leader Training.** Leaders and managers learn the 5 Choices, and also how they can lead their teams in a Q2 way. They are given specific leadership assignments to implement with their teams in the coming five weeks that revolve around the five auditable behaviors described previously.

4. **Team-Member Training.** Teams learn the 5 Choices and are given specific action items to implement within the coming five weeks that revolve around the five auditable behaviors.

5. **Leadership Accountability and Report-Out.** Five weeks after the training, team leaders report to the executive sponsor on their success in implementing the five auditable behaviors and the resulting impact on their team's performance.

6. **Reassessment.** About three months after kickoff, the organization is reassessed in the 5 Choices on how much time is being spent in Q2, as well as assessing the score on the Q2 Energy Index.

7. **Sustainment.** This phase continues for another twelve months and includes continued learning (including onboarding for new hires), implementation tools, pervasive and visible reminders of the material, reassessments, and targeted help where teams are not moving forward as they should.

THE INSTALLATION PROCESS MAP

When the elements of this process are represented visually, it looks like this:

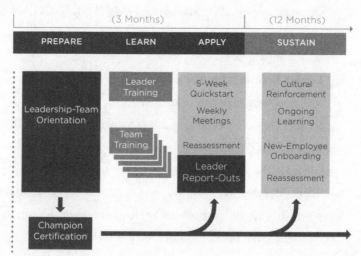

LIMITS OF THE METAPHOR

In all our talk about installing the 5 Choices, we need to be clear that culture can't really be installed. It has to be grown.

While there are clear process steps leaders can follow, it really boils down to the behavior of leaders themselves.

- If leaders are consistently pausing and asking others if they are in Q2, then people will go to Q2.
- If leaders stop themselves publicly before they lob a Q3 at someone, and vocalize what they are doing, then people will do the same thing.
- If leaders talk about the contribution they want to make and share their goals to get there, others will too.
- If leaders are bringing their full energy to work and honor those who do, others will start to do it as well.

Conversely, if leaders violate these behaviors and drive others into Q1 and Q3, others will too, and you will end up with just another flavor-of-the-month initiative, which is, unfortunately, what most people inside organizations have come to expect. It's good for a day, but if the leaders go back to normal, then so will everyone else.

Successful change is an inside-out process of commitment, modeling, and reinforcement carried out by dedicated Q2 leaders.

Becoming a Q2 leader is a win-win proposition, however. Leaders who undertake this path find they are far more productive and fulfilled themselves, and the organizations and people they lead perform better in reaching their most important strategic goals.

THE INSIDE-OUT LEADERSHIP PROCESS FOR BUILDING A Q2 CULTURE

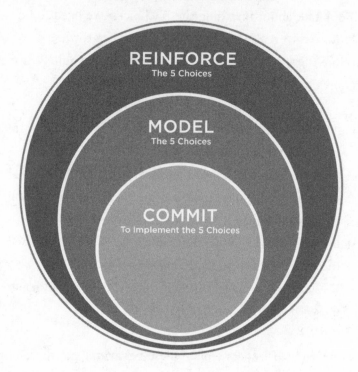

APPENDIX A:
TOP 25 EMAIL PROTOCOLS

1. **Keep it short.** Before you hit Send, look through your email and eliminate everything that doesn't add to your desired outcome.

2. **Make an actionable subject line.** A good subject line is like a good headline—it makes people want to read the rest. If you're sending an email asking someone to do something, put that into your subject line. Example: "Review Budget Documents."

3. **Avoid vague one-word subject lines.** No one wants to read an email lazily titled "Stuff." Be on target as to what the email contains. This also helps to keep the body of your message concise.

4. **Don't discuss more than one subject.** It's called the subject line, not the subjects line. If you have to address more than one topic, send more than one email. Following this practice makes communication easier and helps eliminate lengthy messages

5. **Don't rely on the high-priority indicator (such as "!" or "!!").** What is important to you usually isn't important to others. Sad but true. Use a compelling subject line instead.

6. **Write the body of the email first, before filling in the "To:" line.** We almost instinctively enter the recipient first thing. Try to retrain your brain to have this be the last thing you do. Most people have embarrassed themselves at least once by accidentally sending a message before it was finished. Don't let hitting Send when you meant to hit Attach or Save cost you your career!

7. **List the action steps first.** People tend to read only the first paragraph anyway, even if you have vital information, so don't bury the point of your message at the end.

8. **Be clear about who you're asking to take the actions.** If the message is addressed to more than one person (including ccs) and requests action, list what you are asking each recipient to do. Be specific. Include by when.

    For example:

    To: Paige
    Cc: Mateo, Aldo, Terry

    Paige, would you review the attached document using Track Changes, and have it to proofreading by Friday of this week?

    Terry, Mateo, Aldo, this is FYI: No action for you.

9. **If the message is short, put it in the subject line and put (EOM) at the end.** This stands for "end of message." Using it lets the recipients know they don't need to open the message. You'll be saving everyone time. Example: "The meeting is starting in 15 minutes (EOM)."

10. **Put (NRN) at the end of your message.** This means "no reply needed." Of course, only use this when applicable. People will be silently thanking you.

11. **Use prefixes when necessary.** Writing "Q1" lets people know the urgency of the email and they'll know exactly how they need to respond. But don't cry wolf. Only use Q1 if it really is urgent and important. And if that's the case, is email really the best way to communicate? This brings us to our next point . . .

12. **Don't rely on email for Q1 matters.** Yes, emails are sent within a matter of seconds, but that doesn't guarantee they'll be read within seconds. Don't forget that telephones can still be used to talk directly to one another. Or maybe just getting out of your chair and walking across the hall to have a conversation would be more helpful.

13. **Avoid using too many acronyms.** Acronyms are great time-savers, especially if included in the subject line. But thousands exist, which makes it less likely your reader will know what you're talking about. However, some communication can establish a few common uses in your office. Examples: AR (action required), FYA (for your approval), or QUE (question).

14. **Respond within twenty-four hours.** Of course, this depends on the nature of the email. If it's a Q2 problem that can be addressed later in the week, at least send a message informing the sender when to expect a response.

15. **Don't expect an immediate response.** Since we've advised people to only check their emails at certain parts of their scheduled day, you should be doing the same. So only expect a response within a reasonable amount of time.

16. **Use out-of-office replies.** When you are going to be out for an extended period of time, let people know. You can usually set out-of-office replies for people in your organization, people outside the organization, or both. Some programs let you restrict these replies to people on your contacts list. This is good, because it prevents automatic replies to spam engines, which can increase the amount of spam you receive.

17. **Eliminate unnecessary ccs.** People overuse the cc function daily. Make sure you are only cc'ing people who need to be cc'd. Note that, usually, a cc implies no action is required, but that you are just sharing information. If you want someone in the cc line to take action, make sure to spell it out.

18. **Use bcc very, very carefully.** This is best used when your recipients do not know one another. That way you don't give out anyone's contact information. And some smartphones today may not necessarily show that you were bcc'd, leaving you wide open to reply when you were not seen as one of the recipients. Not good.

19. **Don't use reply all.** You know how low-value most reply alls are . . . stay out of that camp. We thank you, and others will too!

20. **Label your attachments appropriately.** Don't leave recipients guessing which file is which by labeling attachments "document 1.docx" or "CB0056.pdf." Opt for clearer titles. Example: "Minutes From 5/6 Retooling Meeting."

21. **Summarize discussion threads.** If you're forwarding a discussion to another person, it's useful to summarize the discussion rather than having him or her scroll through the entire thing. Or you can highlight only the relevant parts of your message.

22. **Always add new contacts to your address book.** This avoids the risk of a future email getting sent to your junk folder.

23. **Make sure your signature includes contact information.** This helps if someone needs to contact you immediately, or wishes to talk specifics with you through another form of communication.

24. **Don't send emails for private matters.** Work email is not private and is considered company property. Save personal matters for your breaks. Plus, why clutter your valuable email space with personal messages better suited for another account?

25. **Don't use email unless you have to.** Lots of us can get over one hundred messages per day. If you can simply walk down the hall to a co-worker's office, do that. Or if the email takes you more than ten minutes to type, it may be too long for this mode of communication. In general, email works best when used to give and receive information. It is less effective (or even counterproductive) when used to solve conflict, vent, voice strong opinions, gossip, reprimand, or complain. There are better ways to communicate these things . . . or, for some, maybe it's better not to communicate them at all.

APPENDIX B:
KEY MODELS

FRANKLINCOVEY'S TIME MATRIX™

IMPORTANT

Q1 NECESSITY

Crises
Emergency meetings
Last-minute deadlines
Pressing problems
Unforeseen events

Q2 EXTRAORDINARY PRODUCTIVITY

Proactive work
High-impact goals
Creative thinking
Planning
Prevention
Relationship building
Learning and renewal

Q3 DISTRACTION

Needless interruptions
Unnecessary reports
Irrelevant meetings
Other people's minor issues
Unimportant emails, tasks,
phone calls, status posts, etc.

Q4 WASTE

Trivial work
Avoidance activities
Excessive relaxation,
television, gaming, Internet
Time-wasters
Gossip

NOT IMPORTANT

URGENT ⟷ NOT URGENT

FRANKLINCOVEY'S TIME MATRIX™ (BLANK)

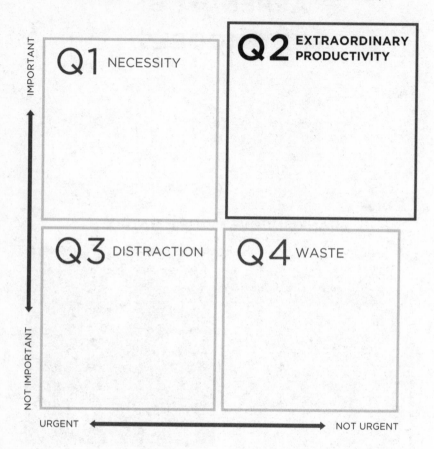

THE Q2 PROCESS™ MAP

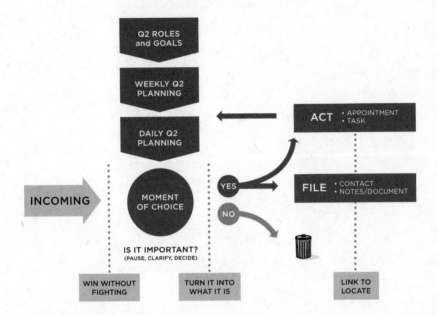

ACKNOWLEDGMENTS

KORY KOGON

A big thank-you to those who made this book possible: my co-author, Adam Merrill, who is a clear model of accomplishment through collaboration and openness, and my other coauthor, Leena Rinne, for her contributions in the development of the content and excellence in facilitating it.

Our reviewers Leigh Stevens, Suzette Blakemore, Jerel McShane, Julie Schmidt, Susan Sabo, Harvey Young, Todd Musig, Elly Rosenthal, Josh Rosenthal, Breck England, Becky Harding, and Andrew Wankier. We tried to keep the review in Q2, but we know it was a little Q1-ish, based on everyone's busy lives and other priorities. We appreciate you fitting us in! And Annie and Zach . . . could not possibly have done this without you!

Lucky for me, I grew up with parents who fostered the conversation around accomplishment every night at the dinner table, always asking us what great things we accomplished or the contribution we made that day. The word *nothing* was not an option. They constantly told us of the potential they saw in us, and they built our muscles around creating value every day. I owe them big-time, as well as my two sisters, Barby Siegel and Elly Rosenthal, with whom the tradition continues.

Last to my partner Pam, who, for over twenty-one years, has been my dose of reality. She works hard to encourage me to keep my eyes on the most important things in life's balance. She has been there time and time again to pull me out from under the gravel when I struggle to say no.

ADAM MERRILL

A big thanks to . . .

Kory Kogon and Leena Rinne. It is a privilege and a blessing to work with two such extraordinary people. I both cherish and relish our work together.

Ben Loehnen, senior editor at Simon & Schuster, along with Brit Hvide, assistant editor, who have been wonderfully visionary and collaborative partners; Barbara Hanson, who undertook the labor of copyediting the manuscript and making it better; and our longstanding and absolutely brilliant agents Jan Miller and Shannon Marven at Dupree/Miller and Associates.

The talented and creative team at FranklinCovey Innovations. I am constantly inspired by your talent, dedication, and commitment—to each other and also to the never-ending challenge of producing truly great products that make a positive difference in the world.

Sean Covey, who leads courageously, acts with integrity, and cares about the details. You are a true leader who inspires greatness.

Scott Miller, who leads FranklinCovey's marketing efforts with extraordinary talent and skill; Annie Oswald, Zach Kristensen, and Jill White, our intrepid book team; Leigh Stevens and Breck

England, who with integrity and commitment work to make everything better; Reid Later, FranklinCovey's editor in chief; our many committed reviewers and research partners in the field, who are committed to the study of human potential; Jody Karr and the FranklinCovey Creative Services team, who collaborated on the book's cover; Santiago Carbonell, who produced the wonderful art and models for this book; and Yvette Richmond, who helped with references and keeps us all running so smoothly.

Masters Bobby and Charlene Lawrence and their family, particularly my primary instructor Dallas Lawrence, for building a family-focused martial arts organization that helps people become goal- and achievement-oriented, while at the same time remaining calm and balanced.

My parents, Roger and Rebecca Merrill, who laid the foundation for this work and everything else in my life and who have given me a lifelong example of positive service and contribution. I am forever grateful.

Julie, my wonderful spouse, and our children: Amy Harrison and her husband, John Harrison; Kimberly, Rachel, and Brandon; and David Harrison, our first grandchild. These individuals teach me daily what extraordinary living is all about and why it all matters.

LEENA RINNE

I'm greatly indebted to the many incredible leaders I've had who have inspired and coached me to go for the extraordinary, including Adam Merrill, Kory Kogon, Sean Covey, Scott Miller, Marianne Phillips, Todd Davis, Catherine Nelson, and Peter Kasic. I also want to express my deep gratitude for the unending support given to me by my sweetheart, David.

ENDNOTES

INTRODUCTION: FEELING BURIED?

1 Grant, Alan W. H. and Leonard A. Schlesinger, "Realize Your Customers' Full Profit Potential." *Harvard Business Review,* September–October 1995, 71.
2 John Medina, "The Brain Rules," *BrainRules.net,* http://brain rules.net/brain-rules-video, Video #1, Exercise.
3. The FranklinCovey Time Matrix study was conducted from 2005 to 2011.

CHOICE 1: ACT ON THE IMPORTANT, DON'T REACT TO THE URGENT

1 Douglas Van Praet, *Unconscious Branding: How Neuroscience Can Empower (and Inspire) Marketing,* New York: Palgrave Macmillan, 2012, 80.
2 Michael Kuhar, Ph.D., *The Addicted Brain: Why We Abuse Drugs, Alcohol, and Nicotine,* Upper Saddle River, NJ: Pearson Education, Inc., 2012, 81.

3 Michael Kuhar, M.D., *The Addicted Brain: Why We Abuse Drugs, Alcohol, and Nicotine,* Upper Saddle River, NJ: Pearson Education, Inc., 2012, 79.

4 Louis Teresi, M.D., *Hijacking the Brain: How Drug and Alcohol Addiction Hijacks Our Brains—The Science Behind Twelve-Step Recovery,* Bloomington, IN: AuthorHouse, 2011, 16.

5 Brené Brown, *Daring Greatly: How the Courage to Be Vulnerable Transforms the Way We Live, Love, Parent, and Lead,* New York: Penguin Group, 2012, 137.

CHOICE 2: GO FOR EXTRAORDINARY, DON'T SETTLE FOR ORDINARY

1 Daniel Amen, M.D., recorded FranklinCovey interview.

2 Daniel H. Pink, *Drive: The Surprising Truth About What Motivates Us,* New York: Penguin Group, 2009, 144–145.

3 Adam Grant, *Give and Take: Why Helping Others Drives Our Success,* New York: Penguin Group, 2013, chapter 6.

4 Heidi Grant Halvorson Ph.D., *Succeed: How We Can Reach Our Goals.* New York: Penguin Group, 2010, 206.

5 Keva Glynn, M.H.A., Heather Maclean, Ed.D., Tonia Forte, M.H.Sc., and Marsha Cohen, M.D., M.H.Sc. "The Association Between Role Overload and Women's Mental Health," *Journal of Women's Health,* vol. 18, p. 2, 2009.

6 Brigid Schulte, *Overwhelmed: Work, Love, and Play When No One Has the Time,* New York: Farrar, Straus and Giroux, 2014, 164.

7 Heidi Grant Halvorson Ph.D., recorded FranklinCovey interview.

8 Daniel H. Pink, *Drive: The Surprising Truth About What Motivates Us,* New York: Penguin Group, Inc., 2009, 138.

CHOICE 3: SCHEDULE THE BIG ROCKS, DON'T SORT GRAVEL

1 Thomas H. Davenport, John C. Beck, *The Attention Economy,* Harvard Business School Press, 2001, 2–3.
2 Heidi Grant Halvorson Ph.D., recorded FranklinCovey interview.
3 Rick Hanson, Ph.D, Richard Mendius, M.D., *Buddha's Brain: The Practical Neuroscience of Happiness, Love, and Wisdom,* Oakland, CA: New Harbinger Publications, Inc., 2009, 200.
4 Heidi Grant Halvorson Ph.D., recorded FranklinCovey interview.
5 Steven R. Covey, *The 7 Habits of Highly Effective People,* New York: Simon & Schuster, 2009, 306.

CHOICE 4: RULE YOUR TECHNOLOGY, DON'T LET IT RULE YOU

1 Herman Kahn, *The Year 2000: A Framework for Speculation on the Next Thirty-three Years,* New York: The Macmillan Company, 1967, 197.
2 Herman Kahn, *The Year 2000: A Framework for Speculation on the Next Thirty-three Years,* New York: The Macmillan Company, 1967, 197.
3 Alex Magdaleno, "Imogen Heap Takes High-Tech Musical Glove to Kickstarter," *Mashable.com,* http://mashable.com/2014/04/11/imogen-heap/.
4 Edward M. Hallowell, M.D., recorded FranklinCovey interview.
5 Catherine Steiner-Adair Ed.D., Teresa H. Barker, *The Big Disconnect: Protecting Childhood and Family Relationships in the Digital Age,* New York: HarperCollins, 2013, 10–11.

6 Catherine Steiner-Adair Ed.D., Teresa H. Barker, *The Big Disconnect: Protecting Childhood and Family Relationships in the Digital Age,* New York: HarperCollins, 2013, 11.

7 Thomas Cleary, *The Japanese Art of War: Understanding the Culture of Strategy,* Boston: Shambhala Publications, 1991, 75.

8 Thomas Cleary, *The Japanese Art of War: Understanding the Culture of Strategy,* Boston: Shambhala Publications, 1991, 77.

9 Julie Morgenstern, *Organizing from the Inside Out,* New York: Henry Holt and Company, 2004, 16.

10 Ed Parker, *Infinite Insights into Kenpo: Mental and Physical Applications,* Los Angeles: Delsby Publications, 1987, xii.

11 "Email Statistics Report, 2014–2018," The Radicati Group, April 2014, p. 4.

12 Sun Tzu, *The Art of War: The Ancient Classic,* West Sussex, United Kingdom: Capstone Publishing (A Wiley Company), 2014, 20.

13 Nick Collins, "Email Raises Stress Levels," telegraph.co.uk, http://www.telegraph.co.uk/science/science-news/10096907/Email-raises-stress-levels.html. You can also check out the related article, "One in Three Workers Suffers from 'Email Stress,'" telegraph.co.uk, http://www.telegraph.co.uk/news/uknews/1560148/One-in-three-workers-suffers-from-email-stress.html.

CHOICE 5: FUEL YOUR FIRE, DON'T BURN OUT

1 Nikhil Swaminathan, "Why Does the Brain Need So Much Power?" *scientificamerican.com,* http://www.scientificamerican.com/article/why-does-the-brain-need-s.

2   Daniel H. Pink, *Drive: The Surprising Truth About What Motivates Us,* New York: Penguin Group, 2009, 78.

3   Daniel H. Pink, *Drive: The Surprising Truth About What Motivates Us,* New York: Penguin Group, 2009, 131.

4   John Ratey, M.D., recorded FranklinCovey interview.

5   John Ratey, M.D., recorded FranklinCovey interview.

6   Christopher Bergland, "The Brain Drain of Inactivity," *psychology today.com,* http://www.psychologytoday.com/blog/the-athletes-way/201212/the-brain-drain-inactivity.

7   Ted Eytan, "The Art of the Walking Meeting," Ted Eytan, M.D., blog, Jan. 10, 2008, http://www.tedeytan.com/2008/01/10/148.

8   John Ratey, M.D., recorded FranklinCovey interview.

9   Joseph Signorile, "Aging and Exercise," *radiowest.kuer.org,* http://radiowest.kuer.org/post/aging-and-exercise.

10   Richard Restack, M.D., recorded FranklinCovey interview.

11   John Ratey, M.D., recorded FranklinCovey interview.

12   Daniel Amen, M.D., recorded FranklinCovey interview.

13   Daniel Amen, M.D., recorded FranklinCovey interview.

14   Joshua Gowin, "Why Your Brain Needs Water," psychologytoday.com, http://www.psychologytoday.com/blog/you-illuminated/201010/why-your-brain-needs-water.

15   Philippa Norman M.D., M.P.H., "Feeding the Brain for Academic Success: How Nutrition and Hydration Boost Learning," healthybrainforlife.com, http://www.healthybrainforlife.com/articles/school-health-and-nutrition/feeding-the-brain-for-academic-success-how.

16   T. Colin Campbell, Thomas M. Campbell II, *The China Study: The Most Comprehensive Study of Nutrition Ever Conducted and the Startling Implications for Diet, Weight Loss and Long-Term Health,* Dallas: BenBella Books, 2006, 228.

17 Thierry Hale, "Rio-Paris Crash, Pilot Fatigue Was Hidden," lepoint.fr, http://www.lepoint.fr/societe/crash-du-rio-paris-la -fatigue-des-pilotes-a-ete-cachee-15-03-2013-1640312_23 .php. There are multiple related accounts, including this one: Robert Mark, "Air France 447 and Sleep Deprivation: A Fatal Link," jetwhine.com, http://www.jetwhine.com/2013/03/af-447 -crash-sleep-deprivation-a-link-appears.

18 Centers for Disease Control, "Insufficient Sleep Is a Public Health Epidemic," cdc.gov, http://www.cdc.gov/features/ds sleep.

19 Liz Joy, M.D., recorded FranklinCovey interview.

20 Alice A. Kuo, "Does Sleep Deprivation Impair Cognitive and Motor Performance as Much as Alcohol Intoxication?" ncbi.nlm .gov, http://www.ncbi.nlm.nih.gov/pmc/articles/PMC1071308.

21 Liz Joy, M.D., recorded FranklinCovey interview.

22 Monica Eng, "Light from electronic screens at night linked to sleep loss," http://articles.chicagotribune.com, http://articles .chicagotribune.com/2012-07-08/news/ct-met-night-light -sleep-20120708_1_blue-light-bright-light-steven-lockley.

23 Monica Eng, "Light from electronic screens at night linked to sleep loss," articles.chicagotribune.com, http://articles.chicago tribune.com/2012-07-08/news/ct-met-night-light-sleep-2012 0708_1_blue-light-bright-light-steven-lockley.

24 William C. Dement, M.D., Ph.D., *The Promise of Sleep: A Pioneer in Sleep Medicine Explores the Vital Connection Between Health, Happiness, and a Good Night's Sleep,* New York: Dell Publishing, 1999, 428.

25 William C. Dement, M.D., Ph.D., *The Promise of Sleep: A Pioneer in Sleep Medicine Explores the Vital Connection Between*

Health, Happiness, and a Good Night's Sleep, New York: Dell Publishing, 1999, 425.

26 William C. Dement, M.D., Ph.D., *The Promise of Sleep: A Pioneer in Sleep Medicine Explores the Vital Connection Between Health, Happiness, and a Good Night's Sleep,* New York: Dell Publishing, 1999, 423.

27 Michael Kellmann, Ph.D., *Enhancing Recovery: Preventing Underperformance in Athletes,* Champaign, IL: Human Kinetics, 2002, vii.

28 Michael Kellmann, Ph.D., *Enhancing Recovery: Preventing Underperformance in Athletes,* Champaign, IL: Human Kinetics, 2002, 5.

29 Sage Roundtree, *The Athlete's Guide to Recovery,* Boulder, CO: Velopress, 2011, 12. Bracketed phrase added.

30 Sage Roundtree, *The Athlete's Guide to Recovery,* Boulder, CO: Velopress, 2011, 13.

31 Sage Roundtree, The Athlete's Guide to Recovery, Boulder, CO, Velopress, 2011, 12.

32 Matt Richtel, "Digital Overload: Your Brain on Gadgets," *Fresh Air,* National Public Radio, Aug. 24, 2010.

33 Phyllis Korkk, "To Stay on Schedule, Take a Break," nytimes.com, http://www.nytimes.com/2012/06/17/jobs/take-breaks-regularly-to-stay-on-schedule-workstation.html?_r=0.

34 Herbert Benson, M.D., Miriam Z. Klipper, *The Relaxation Response,* New York: HarperCollins, 2009, 142–143.

35 Dan Harris, *10% Happier,* New York: HarperCollins, 2014, 170.

36 Natali Moyal, Avishai Henik, Gideon E. Anholt, "Cognitive Strategies to Regulate Emotions—Current Evidence and Future

Directions," journal.frontiersin.org, http://journal.frontiersin
.org/Journal/10.3389/fpsyg.2013.01019/full.

37 Daniel Amen, M.D., recorded FranklinCovey interview.

38 Wikipedia, "Oxytocin," en.wikipedia.org, https://en.wikipedia
.org/wiki/Oxytocin#Fear_and_anxiety_response.

39 Harvard Health Publications, "The health benefits of strong
relationships," health.harvard.edu, http://www.health.harvard
.edu/newsletters/Harvard_Womens_Health_Watch/2010
/December/the-health-benefits-of-strong-relationships.

40 Matthew D. Lieberman, Social: *Why Our Brains Are Wired to
Connect,* New York: Crown Publishing Group, 2013, 58–59.

41 Rebecca Z. Shafir, *The Zen of Listening: Mindful Communication
in the Age of Distraction,* Wheaton, IL: Quest Books, 2012, 243.

42 Louis Cozolino, *The Neuroscience of Human Relationships:
Attachment and the Developing Social Brain,* New York:
W. W. Norton & Company, 2014, 4.

43 Dr. Hallowell, recorded FranklinCovey interview.

WHAT LEADERS CAN DO

1 W. Edwards Deming, brainyquote.com, http://www.brainyquote
.com/quotes/quotes/w/wedwardsd133510.html.

BUILDING A Q2 CULTURE IN YOUR ORGANIZATION

1 Peter F. Drucker, "On knowledge worker productivity," gurteen
.com, http://www.gurteen.com/gurteen/gurteen.nsf/id/X00035
E2A/.

ABOUT THE AUTHORS

KORY KOGON

Kory is FranklinCovey's Global Practice Leader for Productivity, focusing her research and content development around time management, project management, and communication skills. She is one of the authors of *The 5 Choices to Extraordinary Productivity, Project Management Essentials for the Unofficial Project Manager,* and *Presentation Advantage.*

Kory brings over twenty-five years of business expertise from frontline positions to an executive-team member. Prior to FranklinCovey, Kory spent six years as the executive vice president of Worldwide Operations for AlphaGraphics, Inc. She was responsible for the teams and projects that helped franchisees start up their business, develop staff, and reach profitability. She led the implementation of ISO 9000 globally, and managed the installation of the first companywide global learning system.

Kory is well known for her ability to provide the practical application and logic that consistently motivates people to take action. In 2005, *Utah Business Magazine* honored Kory as one of the Business Women to Watch in Utah. In 2012, Kory earned a

Certificate in the Foundations of Neuroleadership from the Neuro-Leadership Institute of which she is an ongoing member.

ADAM MERRILL

Adam Merrill is vice president of Innovations for FranklinCovey, where he leads a group of incredible people in developing award-winning products that help individuals and organizations become dramatically more productive. A lifelong student of innovation, productivity, and leadership, he loves the creative process and working with the talented and committed people that this kind of effort attracts.

Adam has been developing content in the area of time management and productivity for over twenty-five years. In 1994, he was involved in the research that produced *The New York Times* best-selling book *First Things First*, by Stephen R. Covey, A. Roger Merrill, and Rebecca R. Merrill. Over the subsequent two decades, he continued working and researching in this area, paying particular attention to the impact of changing technology on how people succeed in a digital world. He is also deeply interested in the impact of brain science, physical health, and mental energy on one's ability to be productive and make good decisions.

As a busy executive with a variety of responsibilities in and out of the workplace, Adam knows how hard it can be to find the right balance. He makes it work by constantly striving to practice the principles in this book. He fuels his fire by spending time with his family, engaging in community service, spending time outdoors, and practicing the martial arts. He is a third-degree black belt in karate.

Adam earned a bachelor of arts degree in philosophy *magna*

cum laude from Brigham Young University and a master's degree in business administration *with distinction* from the Thunderbird School of Global Management.

LEENA RINNE

Leena Rinne is a senior consultant with FranklinCovey. In this role, she works with clients to increase productivity and develop leaders in their organizations. Leena works with a wide variety of organizations, ranging from Fortune 100 companies to small, locally owned businesses.

Leena has over fifteen years of experience in international business and high-level client relationship management. Currently in her tenth year with FranklinCovey, Leena spent over six years as the international business partner for Europe, the Middle East, and Africa, where she was involved in the corporate strategy planning, operational support, and financial reporting for more than twenty-five FranklinCovey licensed-partner offices. Leena also works with FranklinCovey's Innovations team to develop and launch core productivity and leadership solutions.

Prior to FranklinCovey, Leena worked in management in the telecommunications industry, where she led global operations, as well as the training and development of both new and current employees.

Leena has a master's degree in economics from the University of Utah and lives in Salt Lake City, Utah.

INDEX

FranklinCovey®
THE ULTIMATE COMPETITIVE ADVANTAGE

FranklinCovey is a global, public company specializing in organizational performance improvement. We help organizations and individuals achieve results that require a change in human behavior. Our expertise is in seven areas: leadership, execution, productivity, trust, sales performance, customer loyalty and education. FranklinCovey clients have included 90 percent of the Fortune® 100, more than 75 percent of the Fortune® 500, thousands of small and mid-sized businesses, as well as numerous government entities and educational institutions. FranklinCovey has more than 100 direct and partner offices providing professional services in over 150 countries and territories.

FranklinCovey
ALL ACCESS PASS®

The FranklinCovey All Access Pass provides unlimited access to our best-in-class content and solutions, allowing you to expand your reach, achieve your business objectives, and sustainably impact performance across your organization.

AS A PASSHOLDER, YOU CAN:

- Access FranklinCovey's world-class content, whenever and wherever you need it, including *The 7 Habits of Highly Effective People®: Signature Edition 4.0*, Leading at the *Speed of Trust®*, and *The 5 Choices to Extraordinary Productivity®*.

- Certify your internal facilitators to teach our content, deploy FranklinCovey consultants, or use digital content to reach your learners with the behavior-changing content you require.

- Have access to a certified implementation specialist who will help design impact journeys for behavior change.

- Organize FranklinCovey content around your specific business-related needs.

- Build a common learning experience throughout your entire global organization with our core-content areas, localized into 16 languages.

Join thousands of organizations using the All Access Pass to implement strategy, close operational gaps, increase sales, drive customer loyalty, and improve employee engagement.

To learn more, visit
FRANKLINCOVEY.COM or call **1-888-868-1776**.

FranklinCovey
THE ULTIMATE COMPETITIVE ADVANTAGE

TAKE THE NEXT STEP IN YOUR JOURNEY

PARTICIPATE IN A TWO-DAY *5 CHOICES*® WORK SESSION

Continue your journey toward extraordinary productivity by attending *The 5 Choices to Extraordinary Productivity*® work session. This time- and life-management work session will help you make the right choices as you align your daily and weekly tasks with your own most important goals. You will move from being "buried alive" to extraordinary productivity!

In this two-day experience, you will learn how to:

- Approach each day with an "importance mindset" and identify and eliminate those activities that distract you from achieving your most important goals.
- Define extraordinary outcomes for your roles.
- Create weekly and daily plans that will actually produce your extraordinary outcomes.

To register or for more information, visit
FRANKLINCOVEY.COM/5CWORKSESSION
or call **1-888-868-1776.**

 | American Management Association®

FranklinCovey has partnered with American Management Association® to make this two-day work session available to you Live In-Person or Live Online.